ISSUES THAT CONCERN YOU

Social Networking

Lauri S. Friedman, *Book Editor*

GREENHAVEN PRESS
A part of Gale, Cengage Learning

GALE
CENGAGE Learning™

Detroit • New York • San Francisco • New Haven, Conn • Waterville, Maine • London

GALE
CENGAGE Learning™

Christine Nasso, *Publisher*
Elizabeth Des Chenes, *Managing Editor*

Articles in Greenhaven Press anthologies are often edited for length to meet page requirements. In addition, original titles of these works are changed to clearly present the main thesis and to explicitly indicate the author's opinion. Every effort is made to ensure that Greenhaven Press accurately reflects the original intent of the authors. Every effort has been made to trace the owners of copyrighted material.

Cover image Supri Suharjoto/Shutterstock.com.

LIBRARY OF CONGRESS CATALOGING-IN-PUBLICATION DATA
Social networking / Lauri S. Friedman, book editor.   p. cm. -- (Issues that concern you) Includes bibliographical references and index. ISBN 978-0-7377-5135-2 (hbk.) 1. Online social networks. I. Friedman, Lauri S. HM742.S6293 2011 302.30285--dc22
2011006024

Printed in the United States of America
2 3 4 5 6 7 15 14 13 12 11

CONTENTS

In December 2010 Mark Zuckerberg, founder of the social networking giant Facebook, was named *Time* magazine's Person of the Year. The highly coveted accolade was by no means undeserved: Zuckerberg is the youngest billionaire on the planet, worth an estimated $7 billion, more than Apple founder Steve Jobs or Google CEO Eric Schmidt. By the end of that year, reported *Time*, more than 550 million people had an account at his website, which he created out of his Harvard dorm room in 2004. That is more than the population of the entire European Union (which by mid-2010 was just over 500 million) and nearly twice that of the United States (whose population as of early 2011 was about 310 million). In 2011 Facebook's community was growing at a rate of about seven hundred thousand people per day. If it were a real nation, it would be the third most populous on earth.

Zuckerberg's site, along with other social networking sites such as Xanga, Bebo, Orkut, Ning, Habbo, LinkedIn, and many others, has irrefutably connected many of the world's citizens (about one in every twelve people on the planet has a Facebook account; one in six Americans has a LinkedIn account). What is more in debate is whether social networking sites have improved the quality of human communications and whether they spawn or stifle the kind of critical thinking and idea-hatching that has been the hallmark of previous communication revolutions.

Though often used for superficial purposes, Facebook, Twitter, and other social networking sites have also championed very serious endeavors, such as inspiring political revolutions or influencing the outcome of elections. During the 2008 presidential campaign, for example, then-senator Barack Obama made masterful use of social networking platforms to electrify voters and catapult himself to the presidency. During the campaign Obama used more than fifteen social networking sites—including MySpace,

Facebook, BlackPlanet (a social networking site for African Americans), and Eons (a site for Americans in their fifties and sixties)—to gain more than 5 million supporters. Since becoming president, more than 17 million have linked to him on Facebook and more than 6 million people follow him on Twitter.

The intense interest in—and ultimate election of—Obama stemmed directly from his use of social networking media. "The Obama campaign did not invent anything completely new," writes *New York Times* reporter David Carr. "Instead, by bolting together social networking applications under the banner of a movement, they created an unforeseen force to raise money, organize locally, fight smear campaigns and get out the vote."[1] Lawyer Ranjit Mathoda points out that Obama is part of a select group of influential politicians who embraced the technology of their day in a unique and visionary way. "Thomas Jefferson used newspapers to win the presidency, F.D.R. [Franklin Delano Roosevelt] used radio to change the way he governed, J.F.K. [John F. Kennedy] was the first president to understand television, and [2004 Democratic presidential hopeful] Howard Dean saw the value of the Web for raising money," says Mathoda. "But Senator Barack Obama understood that you could use the Web to lower the cost of building a political brand, create a sense of connection and engagement, and dispense with the command and control method of governing to allow people to self-organize to do the work."[2] Indeed, Obama's visionary use of social networking applications secured him the presidency and established him as a twenty-first-century Web-savvy politician.

Yet others disagree that social networking sites have enriched human communication or made any positive contribution to society. In fact, some argue that such sites have impoverished communication by encouraging thoughts that are too pithy, short, or superficial to constitute any meaningful contribution to human development. Neal Gabler, writing in the *Los Angeles Times*, describes social networking communications as "haiku-like" for the way in which they primitively force users to distill their thoughts down to the most basic nouns and verbs and to limit their ideas to a couple hundred characters or less. "The more we text and

In December 2010 Mark Zuckerberg, founder of Facebook, was named Time *magazine's Person of the Year.*

Twitter and 'friend,'" writes Gabler, "the less likely we are to have the habit of mind or the means of expressing ourselves in interesting and complex ways."[3] He compares Zuckerberg's Facebook revolution to another communication revolution—Johannes Gutenberg's invention of the printing press in the mid-1400s. This revolutionary invention allowed, for the first time in human history, ideas to be communicated and disseminated to the masses. As a result, it spurred an outpouring of immensely valuable artistic, political, and scientific thought. "Gutenberg's Revolution left us with a world that was intellectually rich," says Gabler. In contrast, "Zuckerberg's portends one that is all thumbs and no brains."[4]

Whether social networking has enriched or impoverished human communications is a matter of opinion; yet the magnitude of social networking, and its status as the twenty-first century's premier mode of interaction, is now established fact. The effect social networking has had on relationships, journalism, and politics are just some of the issues explored in *Issues That Concern You: Social Networking*. Readers will find much to consider in pro-con pairs of articles that examine how this fast-changing phenomenon is affecting all sectors of society.

Notes

1. David Carr, "How Obama Tapped into Social Networks' Power," *New York Times*, November 9, 2008, p. B1.
2. Quoted in Carr, "How Obama Tapped into Social Networks' Power."
3. Neal Gabler, "The Zuckerberg Revolution," *Los Angeles Times*, November 28, 2010. www.latimes.com/news/opinion/commentary/la-oe-gabler-zuckerberg-20101128,0,7889675.story.
4. Gabler, "The Zuckerberg Revolution."

ONE

Social Networking Improves Human Relationships

Richard Banfield

> Online social networks tap into a base need of humans to connect with others, argues Richard Banfield in the following viewpoint. Banfield rejects claims that social networking and social media are making people stupid or more isolated. In Banfield's opinion, just the opposite is true: Social networking keeps people connected to their communities near and far. Connections made online often result in real-world meetings, he says. Social networking also allows people to valuably expand their social horizons—both professionally and personally. For all of these reasons, Banfield concludes that social networking improves and facilitates human relationships.
>
> Banfield owns a Boston Web design consultancy called Fresh Tilled Soil.

Apparently social media is making us less sociable and stupid. From the writings of marketing consultant Faith Popcorn to the recent University of Southern California study on the effects of spending time on the web, we've been led to believe that surfing the web and social network is eating away at our abilities to be human. In a number of articles, tweets and posts I have read recently there is a lot of concern about how social media

Richard Banfield, "In Defense of Social Networking: A Friend Is Still a Friend," *Mass High Tech: The Journal of New England Technology*, May 15, 2009. Reprinted by permission.

makes us lazy social beings and shuts us off from the "real world." Apparently, we have so much access to online strangers that we now don't need to connect to our real-life friends in real-world situations. According to these authors we're headed for a world where we have no privacy, no friends, and a mental state equivalent to a chocolate sundae.

Reasons to Be Optimistic About Social Networking

I'm more optimistic about the web and the effects of social networking. Virtual connection with friends on Facebook and Twitter doesn't make me less social, it makes me more social. Just because the medium or channel is different doesn't make it less social.

Humans are wired to be social. In a recent article by Atul Gawande in the *New Yorker*, Gawande points to several studies that prove we are fundamentally attracted to situations that connect us to other people. Solitary confinement or even self-imposed "cocooning" is as detrimental to your brain as physical brain trauma and we are wired to avoid those situations.

Social media allows us to make connections, however small, to remind ourselves we're part of a much bigger society. We can solve bigger problems through connections even when they are only "tweets" or comments on a blog. These micro-social engagements also lead to more old-fashioned socializing. Through Twitter, I have discovered several local web innovation events, like Mass Innovators and Refresh Boston, that I've been attending in the company of other real people. I've also been connected to dozens of new clients and business partners. Twitter now accounts for most of the new traffic to our website and many of our clients. Those are real-world connections with real-world advantages.

We Should Not Be Afraid of Sharing Ourselves

Social network privacy, or the lack thereof, is the biggest distraction ever concocted by web critics. If two thirds of our brain is dedicated to making social connections to other humans, then why is there such a concern with privacy? Who are we trying to protect?

Virtual connections with friends on Facebook may make people more social by expanding their professional and personal horizons.

Breaking down barriers to information helps make us smarter. We make better decisions when we know more about the people we meet. Googling a potential client or a new friend helps me get a deeper understanding of their backgrounds and their personalities.

I don't buy the argument that a lack of privacy endangers our children either. There have always been crimes against strangers; the only difference is that now we can see what's been going on

Social Networking Brings People Together

A 2007 study found that most Facebook users said people they already know are the prime viewers of their profile page. This supports the idea that social networks serve to enhance the in-person relationships people already have.

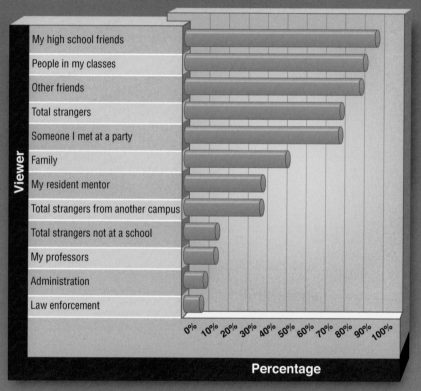

Taken from: Nicole B. Ellison, Charles Steinfield, and Cliff Lampe, "The Benefits of Facebook 'Friends': Social Capital and College Students' Use of Online Social Network Sites," Michigan State University, 2007.

behind closed doors. Hiding behind the privacy argument is ostrich mentality. This is not to say you shouldn't use parental controls to keep your 6-year-old from stumbling on a porn site. That's a no-brainer. But we also need to stop pretending that this is something that we can control. The privacy horse bolted a long time ago and our job is to understand how to make it a positive force.

Not avoiding the truth but rather focusing that energy of abundant information makes us the smart ones.

Social Networks Are Important Tools

The bottom line is your brain wouldn't have evolved its huge socializing frontal cortex if connecting to other human beings weren't a primary driver of successful evolution.

Connecting is what we do. The great social experiment is not in the details of how we connect but that we are connecting more than we have ever before. Connections make us smarter, at a neurological level and at an ecological level. I really don't need to have another scientific study to know that connecting to more people is better. It's written in my genes. I wouldn't even be here if it weren't for the fundamental evolutionary drive to connect. My entire existence is about socializing with or without the web. I'm just very fortunate that I live in a time when connecting is so much faster and easier. I'm smarter because of the social web, and I look forward to getting smarter.

TWO

Social Networking Threatens Human Relationships

Madeleine Bunting

> Social media and modern technology threaten to erode human relationships, argues Madeleine Bunting in the following viewpoint. She explains that as humans become more obsessed with cell phones, computers, and other means of social media, they lose the ability to read each other's body language, communicate with each other, and make important commitments to one another. Each of these is critical for building lasting and deep relationships, says Bunting. She cites studies that show today's young people are lonelier and more socially isolated than those of the past. Bunting says this is because social media are replacing and reshaping the relationships people make with one another, and this is a significant concern.
>
> Bunting is a columnist for the *Guardian*, the Manchester, United Kingdom, newspaper in which this viewpoint was originally published. She writes on a wide range of subjects including politics, work, Islam, science and ethics, development, women's issues, and social change.

In the two weeks leading up to Christmas, the crisis of environmental sustainability dominated every headline. Since the new year, a number of stories seem to raise disturbing questions about another kind of sustainability: the durability and quality of human relationships, and how we transmit to children the skills and values needed to conduct them. There have been a batch of stories about loneliness; we now have well-established evidence of rising depression rates and increased emotional problems in adolescence. In his fascinating book *Loneliness*, John Cacioppo, the American psychologist, argues that one-fifth of people are lonely.

There is no shortage of explanations as to the causes of this unhappy fifth. Interestingly, two of the most popular—family breakdown favoured by the right and inequality favoured by the left—were largely ruled out in one of the most meticulous time trend studies of this growing malaise. The Nuffield Foundation's groundbreaking work on adolescence, which now spans 1974 to 2004, is unequivocal that young people in the UK now have a "significantly higher level of emotional and behavioural problems than 16-year-olds living through the 70s and 80s". But it dismissed "fractured" family lives as a cause and was clear that "increasing socio-economic inequalities are not the full explanation". It asks: "Has something changed about peer group interactions and non-family socialisation? Do young people spend their time in very different ways compared with their parents' generation? Do they spend less time with adults? Do we parent differently from families in other countries or differently from the 70s?"

The short answer to all of the above is yes. The most obvious driver of change is new media technology, which is dramatically re-shaping all kinds of human interaction. Raymond Tallis has coined the word the "e-ttenuation" of relationships to describe the consequences: faced with such an abundance of interesting choices, there is a reluctance to commit and a provisionalism which promotes grazing, keeping options open. Above all, there is a paradigm of contractualism: relationships are measured by the question "what's in it for me?" It is not technology per se at fault, but how it is used, and in particular how it combines with another equally powerful phenomenon—commercialisation; the assessment that everyone and everything has a price. It is the two combined which I would argue are so corrosive to our capabilities to create and sustain relationships of depth and durability.

The author claims that children spend an average of six hours a day in front of screens at the expense of face-to-face interaction with friends and family members.

Last week's report by Jean Gross, an educational psychologist, that one in six children has difficulty learning to speak and listen, is the kind of story which gets likened to the canary down the mine shaft. It follows several reports with similar findings: children are turning up to primary school struggling to construct sentences, according to John Bercow's government report in 2008.

The process of listening to someone and responding in speech is the most ordinary everyday task—and the most demanding of social skills. How we read facial expressions, body language and speech to interpret what has been said, and how that expresses relationships, is an immensely complex process. Listening is a huge, much underrated skill, requiring personal preoccupations to be set aside, if only momentarily, in order to be attentive to another.

These skills are among the most important inheritance a parent ever bequeaths; if these are not being transmitted effectively in a significant section of the population, what is going on? Gross pointed to factors such as parents not having enough time with their children because of long working hours, and too much screen-based entertainment. The child needs you, "not expensive toys and big houses", concluded Gross.

Children are spending on average six hours a day in front of screens—either computers or televisions. Interaction with their parents is subject to interruptions from mobiles and BlackBerrys as work spills into private lives. Increasingly the rarest experience in family life is undivided attention, being *present* as everyone juggles technologies: iPods and Facebook, BlackBerrys and landlines. Family life is no longer private, it's porous to all the networks outside it.

iPods can be great, mobile phones very useful, and it's handy keeping up with people on Facebook. The problem is the quantity of this connectivity and its potential for addiction—how it is deliberately designed to draw people ever deeper. A majority of people can put boundaries on these pleasures—even Davina McCall, who has presided over a particularly addictive form of reality television, rations TV for her three children, we were told last week. But that requires a form of self-control, and deferred gratification—values which are profoundly counter-cultural and yet which psychologists argue are crucial life skills: you learn them if you are lucky enough to have parents who understand their importance and teach them by example. That's a lottery.

The potential damage of the "telemediation" of everyday life is compounded by the fact that so much of screen entertainment is commercialised. It's a world increasingly structured around buying and selling; the average viewer sees 43 adverts a day compared with

33 a decade ago. The internet is permeated with desperate, intrusive salesmanship. Adults have slowly been allowed to develop the capacity to deal with advertising; children stumble into these network shopping malls bewildered. With a tin ear for this issue, the culture secretary, Ben Bradshaw, announced last week to howls of outrage that the government will allow product placement in television programmes. Another precious bastion of public space beyond the tentacles of commercialisation is collapsing.

If you want to glimpse how children are being groomed to operate in this commercialised telemediated space, go to Club Penguin. Kids are enthralled by its elaborate world of puffles and dojos; seduced on to a free site, the child is then confronted at every point by options reserved for fully paid-up members. The latter get to decorate their igloos and change the clothes on their penguin avatar. This is a game which trains children to understand how consumerism humiliates and excludes those who can't pay.

Children graduate from Club Penguin to Facebook, where adolescents have found a whole new forum for their quest for selfhood. "Who am I, who do I want to be?": these staples of western individualism have found amplification on the net. As an article in the New York Times explored, social networking is curiously addictive as it feeds on adolescent social insecurities. One social scientist argued: "If you're watching the social landscape on the screen and if you're obsessed with your position in that landscape, it's very hard to look away."

This is not a Luddite diatribe against technology, but an argument for how carefully it has to be managed if other human attributes, such as the capacity for commitment, are to flourish. The American academic Robert Putnam, in his influential book *Bowling Alone*, placed considerable blame on television for the decline in many aspects of civic engagement. We should be watching carefully for how a new generation of media technology might erode another area of relationship—the intimacies of family life, the nursery of our skills to speak, listen and build relationships.

THREE

Social Networks Boost Users' Self-Esteem and Sense of Belonging

Kine Dorum, Craig Bartle, and Martin Pennington

Kine Dorum, Craig Bartle, and Martin Pennington are researchers with the Student Retention and Success Project, an organization based at the University of Leicester, United Kingdom, that studies the role of belonging and intimacy in facilitating student success and satisfaction. In the following viewpoint they argue that students who use social networking sites have a higher sense of belonging than students who do not. They offer study results that show that students who use online social networks such as Facebook are better integrated into their community, feel more positive about their community, are better settled into university life, and more in touch with events on campus than students not using social networks. Social networks also helped students who live off campus feel connected to their schools. The authors conclude that online networking sites act as a social glue that keeps young people critically interconnected.

Going to university is for most students both an exciting and daunting experience. Students face many new challenges such as meeting new people, making friends, living away from home, and taking on academic responsibilities. It is also an important part of the transition to adulthood for an increasing number of young people. According to the Higher Education Statistics Agency (HESA) the number of students accepted on to courses at British universities passed 500,000 in 2009. During this transition stage, the degree to which students feel they belong to the institution at which they are enrolled can have a significant impact on their overall experience of university life, satisfaction, and academic attainment.

A Sense of Belonging Is Critical for Young People

Many educational researchers are in agreement that the sense of belonging, or the cohesion a student has with a particular institution, is one of the most important requirements to ensure individuals' proper functioning within a learning environment. Social integration is consistently found to impact student persistence, and developing valued relationships is an important part of that integration. Studies show that attrition often occurs among first year students who have not been integrated into the campus community. The present study is part of a larger project funded by the Paul Hamlyn Foundation and the Higher Education Funding Council for England (HEFCE) investigating antecedents [circumstances occurring prior to entering university] and effects of sense of belonging among students at the University of Leicester, UK.

Undergraduate student persistence is a broadly studied topic within the field of higher education studies. Key in this work is the research of [Vincent] Tinto. Focusing on institutional structural factors, Tinto's theory posits that early withdrawal is impacted by a variety of factors. As students come into an institution, they do so with a variety of backgrounds, intents, and commitments. On arrival, two key concepts affect persistence: academic and social integration. If students are not well integrated into the university or college environment, they are at increased risk of withdrawing. . . .

Facebook Helps Students Adjust to College

[Researchers C.] Madge, [J.] Meek, [J.] Wellens and [T.] Hooley conducted an investigation into the role of online social networking sites (specifically Facebook) in first year students' settling in to

Most American Teens Use a Social Networking Site

The majority of American teens have at least one profile on a social networking site.

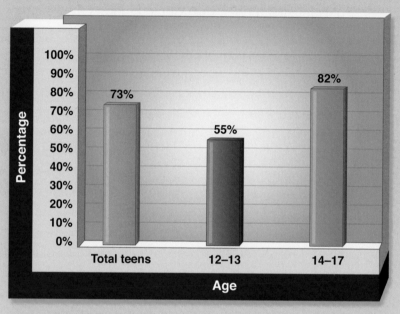

Taken from: Pew Internet, September 2009.

academic and social life. In a survey of 221 students they found that more than half (55 per cent) had joined Facebook to make new friends prior to entering university, while a further 43 per cent joined immediately after starting university. Nearly three quarters of the respondents said Facebook had played an important part in helping them to settle in at university. Specifically, students preferred using Facebook for social reasons, rather than for formal teaching and administrative purposes. It was concluded that Facebook functions as a 'social glue' that helps students settle into university life, that keeps the student body together as a community, and aids in communication (especially about social events) within the student body. However, it was also stressed that Facebook is only *one* aspect of students' social networking practices and clearly face-to-face relationships and interactions remain significant.

Social Networking Sites Act as a "Social Glue"

The above theoretical perspectives indicate that social interaction and integration are key elements in students' developing a sense of belonging to their institution. Findings showing that students living off campus are at a social disadvantage suggest that it is important to identify ways of promoting social interaction and information sharing among this particular group. The idea of online social networking sites as 'social glue' is something that can be tapped into as a tool for encouraging social integration and information sharing among students who spend less time in face-to-face interaction with their peers. It was predicted that students' living arrangements would have a significant effect of self-reported sense of belonging; specifically that off-campus students would report significantly lower sense of belonging than on-campus students. It was also predicted that the use of social networking sites would have a significant effect on self-reported sense of belonging among off-campus students. Lastly, it was predicted that there would be a significant positive relationship between sense of belonging and general attitudes towards university life. . . .

Results revealed significant effects of term-time accommodation arrangements and making friends via online social networking sites on sense of belonging scores. Students living on campus reported significantly higher sense of belonging than students living off campus; this was also the case for students who had made friends online compared to those who had not. A significant interaction effect indicated that the effect of living on or off campus diminished when accounting for use of social networking sites; in other words, off-campus students who had made friends online reported higher sense of belonging than off-campus students who had not. For on-campus students making friends online did not make a significant difference to their sense of belonging. Results also showed there was a significant relationship between scores on the attitude scale and self-reported sense of belonging, in that positive

A survey among college students reveals that 43 percent joined Facebook after they started college, and 55 percent had joined before they started.

attitude was associated with stronger sense of belonging. Further analyses showed that accommodation and social networking also had an effect on attitudes in a similar way to sense of belonging. Sense of belonging was significantly related to social, academic and personal aspects of attitudes.

Social Networking Sites Increase Sense of Belonging

The findings with regards to sense of belonging among off-campus students correspond to those of previous studies. Students who live on campus are at an advantage in that they are physically present where information about social activities is being shared, in addition to having easier access to social support from peers and accommodation staff. This in turn aids group cohesion and forming of social bonds. Students living off campus reported lower sense of belonging, which can be attributed to them spending less time interacting with peers, and thus experience less of the social inclusion and cohesion of on-campus students. The notion of online social networking sites acting as a social facilitator is strengthened by the findings with respect to off-campus students. Although not a replacement for face-to-face interaction, online social networking is of increased importance to this group, and can help reduce the social and informational disadvantage experienced by off-campus students.

Sense of belonging was strongly related to general attitudes, a finding which emphasises the importance of this particular aspect of the student experience. Sense of belonging and attitudes were affected similarly by accommodation and use of social networking sites. Perhaps contrary to Madge and colleagues' suggestion, the use of social networking sites was associated with positive attitudes to academic aspects of student life, as well and social and personal aspects. This could perhaps be explained by a positive 'carry over' effect of using social networking sites. Even if the sites are not used for academic purposes *per se*, developing social bonds and cultivating a sense of belonging results in more positive attitudes. Positive attitudes, in turn, are related to increased academic attainment and adjustment. . . . The measure of sense of belonging used in this study was of a general nature, and at this point it is difficult to draw causal conclusions [definitively show what causes a sense of belonging] about the relationship between sense of belonging and attitudes. It is, however, clear that cultivating a sense of belonging is of overall benefit to the individual student. Sense of belonging is a multifaceted concept, and thus very difficult to define. Drawing on the present findings it might be useful in future research to adopt a more individual approach to the topic in order to gain an understanding of what the individual student sees as important for their sense of belonging to an institution, and how this translates to their use of online social networking sites.

FOUR

Social Networks Increase Antisocial Behavior

Charlotte Steinway

Social networking cultivates antisocial behavior, argues Charlotte Steinway in the following viewpoint. Steinway describes how on her college campus, students hide behind Facebook and their cell phones, rather than acknowledging each other in person. She says it is common for students to ignore each other when they pass on campus. Some even pretend to text or be on the phone when they walk around school so they have an excuse not to talk to each other. Yet the same students, says Steinway, willingly interact with each other online. Steinway thinks this is unacceptable and abnormal. She says all humans have a duty to be social and encourages her fellow students not to be afraid to befriend each other in real life.

Steinway is a contributor to *Red: Teenage Girls in America Write on What Fires Up Their Lives Today*. She was a senior at Tufts University when she wrote this article for the *Boston Globe*.

There's a silent epidemic making the rounds at my college. No one talks about it because, quite literally, it goes unspoken.

When I first set foot on campus, I feared every freshman's pariah nightmare was coming true: Kids who had friend-requested

It is common for students to ignore one another in person but to text each other.

me on Facebook [FB] were pretending I didn't exist when I passed them on the quad. People from my wilderness pre-orientation— people I'd shared sleeping bags with only a couple weeks earlier— would look at me, then immediately look away. A girl I'd given my lecture notes to walked right by as if I were a stranger. But a dozen or so conversations with friends and classmates led me to realize it wasn't me alone being shunned.

Hiding Behind Our Gadgets

No, I was getting the cold backpacked shoulder largely because everyone was on their iPod or cellphone, or at least pretending to be. The elderly use canes, the youth use phones. What horrified me the most was that by the end of September, I was right there with them, pretending I didn't recognize the kid whose Facebook page told me he too likes [the bands] TV on the Radio and Ratatat. And I was clutching my phone with a severity of object attachment I hadn't felt since the days of the pacifier. In an age where hookups, breakups, and makeups are increasingly initiated via text or online, the social dynamic of face-to-face interactions has changed drastically and in some cases disappeared entirely.

As a sociology major and a member of this be-everywhere-now generation, I find the silence deadening. Also, if it's this bad on a college campus—where our lives are landscaped to criss-cross each other many times a day—what happens when we graduate and retreat into separate cities, homes, cars, marriages? One friend, a junior who's on the shy side, told me she relies heavily on her electronic escape hatch. "I'll walk by someone, I'll have my iPod in, even if it's not on, and they'll think I didn't say hi because I was distracted. So it gives me an excuse."

An Obsession with Appearing in Demand Results in Loneliness

Another classmate admits she's turned to "fauxting," fake texting when she realizes that someone she knows is about to actively ignore her. Given an option, there isn't a college student out there who will choose to invite rejection. "Everyone wants everyone else to say hi but doesn't want to be the person saying hi," as my housemate put it. We use cellphones to mediate the way others perceive us; if we're texting or calling a friend, we appear sought after, occupied, in demand.

But the tragic, isolating thing is that we reach for our devices because we don't want to seem lonely—which is causing us to avoid our peers and actually be lonely.

We Have a Human Duty to Be Social

In 1983, Erving Goffman, a founder of the symbolic interactionist school of sociology, claimed that humans of "acquaintanceship" are enlisted to "the right and obligation mutually to . . . acknowledge individual identification on all initial occasions of incidentally produced proximity." In English, this means that every time you happen to be within physical range of someone you know, it is your duty as a social being to acknowledge this person, ideally with a hello followed by their name.

Oh, how we now scoff at the Goff. I can't count the number of times I've talked to someone at a party, promising to start saying hi to each other on campus. The next morning, we pass on the way to class—and *nothing*.

The precedent is set. And I'm sick of it. Um, hello? Start saying it. If you don't know the name of someone you recognize, use the tools you've got (FB) to figure it out. If they reject your greeting, well, then you really have something to text your friend about. I was recently at a party and got to talking to a boy I'd seen around but had never spoken to. The next day, when we passed on the quad and gave each other that "Are you going to say hi?" look, I vowed to break the silence.

"Hey Matt, what's up?" I said. Only slightly startled, he replied with "Hey" and a smile. A couple hours later he friend-requested me on Facebook.

FIVE

Social Networking Can Cultivate True Friendships

Kate Dailey

Online friends qualify as true friends, argues journalist Kate Dailey in the following viewpoint. She says the experience of being friends on a social network like Facebook mimics many of the qualities of in-person friendships. Such relationships offer people the opportunity to listen to one another, help each other through difficult times, pay attention to life events, and offer positive reinforcement and congratulations. Online friendships can also remove some of the awkwardness of in-person interactions and allow people to not limit their friendships by geography. Dailey acknowledges that online friendships lack some of the closeness that in-person ones have, but says they are better than nothing. She concludes that online friendships should be encouraged because they provide much of the same emotional support that in-person friendships do.

I have a friend named Sue. Actually, "Sue" isn't her real name, and she isn't really a friend: she's something akin to a lost sorority sister—we went to the same college, participated in the same activities and had a lot of mutual respect and admiration for one another. But since graduation, we've fallen out of touch, and the only way I know about Sue, her life and her family is through her Facebook updates. That's why I felt almost like a voyeur when Sue announced, via Facebook, the death of her young son. I was surprised she had chosen to share something so personal online—and then ashamed, because since when did I become the arbiter of what's appropriate for that kind of grief?

The more I thought about it, the more I realized Facebook might be the perfect venue for tragic news: it's the fastest way to disseminate important information to the group without having to deal with painful phone calls; it allowed well-meaning friends and acquaintances to instantly pass on condolences, which the family could read at their leisure, and it eliminated the possibility that were I to run into Sue in the supermarket, I'd ask unknowingly about her son and force her to replay the story over again.

Facebook Friends Count as Real Friends

Numerous studies have shown that a strong network of friends can be crucial to getting through a crisis, and can help you be healthier in general. But could virtual friends, like the group of online buddies that reached out to Sue, be just as helpful as the flesh-and-blood versions? In other words, do Facebook friends— and the support we get from them—count? These questions are all the more intriguing as the number of online social-network users increase. Facebook attracted 67.5 million visitors in the U.S. in April, and the fastest-growing demographic is people over 35. It's clear that connecting to friends, both close and distant, via the computer will become more the norm than novelty.

Researchers have yet to significantly study the social implications of Facebook, so what we do know is gleaned from general studies about friendship, and some of the emerging studies about online networking. First, a definition of "friends": In research circles, experts define a friend as a close, equal, voluntary partnership—though Rebecca G. Adams, a professor of sociology at the University of North Carolina, Greensboro, says that in reality, "friendships don't have to be equal or close, and we know from research that friendships aren't as voluntary as they seem," because they're often constricted by education, age and background.

Friends on Facebook seem to mimic, if not replicate, this trend—there are people online that you are more likely to chat with every day, while others only make an appearance once or twice a year, content to spend the rest of the time residing silently in your friend queue. (Though the Facebook friends with whom you have frequent social interaction might not be people you interact with often in "real life.")

In life, having 700 people in your circle of friends could get overwhelming, but that's less of an issue online. "Research suggests that people are only intermittently in touch with many of their online 'friends' but correspond regularly with only a few good friends," says Shelley E. Taylor, professor of psychology at the University of California, Los Angeles. "That said, creating networks to ease the transition to new places can be hugely helpful to people, offsetting loneliness until new friends are made."

Social Networks Are Social Lifelines

In other words, Facebook may not replace the full benefits of real friendship, but it definitely beats the alternative. I conducted a very informal poll via my Facebook status update, asking if Facebook makes us better friends. A high-school pal, with whom I haven't spoken in about 10 years, confessed that since she had her baby, corresponding via Facebook has been a lifeline—and even if she wasn't actively commenting, it was nice to know what people were up to. "Any electronic communication where you don't have to be in the same physical space is going to decrease feelings of isolation," says Dr. Adams.

Several people in my online network admit that Facebook doesn't make them a better friend, but a better acquaintance, more likely to dash off a quick happy birthday e-mail, or to comment on the photo of a new puppy. But that's not a bad thing. Having a large group of "friends" eager to comment on your daily life could be good for your self-esteem. When you get a new job, a celebratory lunch with your best friends will make you feel good and make for a fantastic memory. But the boost you get from the 15 Facebook friends who left encouraging comments can also make you happy.

Online friendships can provide much of the same emotional support that in-person friendships do.

"The way to think of this is before the Internet, we wouldn't see our acquaintances very often: every once in a while, we might show up at a wedding and suddenly have 100 of our closest friends around," says James Fowler, associate professor of political science at the University of California, San Diego. "With Facebook, it's like every day is a wedding." And just like leaving a wedding may leave you feeling energized and inspired by reconnecting to old pals, so can spending time on Facebook," says Fowler.

People Find Solace in Their Online Friendships

While Fowler's research also shows that bad habits like smoking and weight gain can be contagious among close friends, emotions like happiness and sadness are easily transferable through acquaintances. The good news? "Because happiness spreads more easily than unhappiness, getting positive comments from your Facebook friends is more likely to make you happy than sad," he says.

Shy people who may not always be able to engage friends in the real world are finding solace in the structure of Facebook. Though people who identify as shy have a smaller circle of Facebook friends than those who don't, they are better able to engage with the online friends they do have. "Because people don't have to interact face-to-face, that's why we're seeing them having relationships: they can think more about what they have to say and how they want to say it," says Craig Ross, a graduate student in psychology at the University of Windsor who studies online social networks.

And what of my "friend" "Sue"? Can the support she received from Facebook friends upon learning about the death of her son replicate the support that would come from friends stopping by the house? It's impossible to replace the warm feelings—or brain-boosting endorphins—that come from human-on-human contact, and you can't send someone a casserole through Facebook. But grieving online can have powerful and productive benefits. Diana Nash, professor of psychology at Marymount Manhattan College, who has studied how college students use MySpace to deal with grief, notes that, "One of the primary desires that we all have is for someone to really listen to us in a deep kind of way. They want to be listened to," she says. Her research shows that by sharing their grief on MySpace, her subjects felt more listened to and more visible, and doing so helped them heal.

Posting personal experiences, no matter how painful, also allows acquaintances who have lived through similar experiences to reach out, either with information about support groups or just an empathetic ear. "The idea of sharing a commonality helps make it a little more bearable. You're not alone, and there are others going through what you went through," says Nash. "It doesn't take away the pain, but it can lessen the pain and make you feel not so alone."

Online Friendship Not Perfect but Still Valuable

The majority of times we reach out on Facebook, however, it's not about a tragedy, but a smaller problem for which we need advice: good movers in the San Francisco area, a copy of yesterday's newspapers, answers to a question about taxes. This is another place where the large Facebook networks come in handy. In real life, people tend to befriend people who think thoughts and live very similar lives to their own, but because on Facebook people often "friend" classmates, people met at parties, and friends-of-friends, the networks include individuals who wouldn't make the "real friend" cut. Having that diversity of opinion and experience available online increases the diversity of responses received when posting a question, which allows you to make a better-informed decision.

Still, there are experts who worry that too much time online keeps us from living satisfying lives in the real world. "It's great to have a lot of Facebook friends, but how many of those friends will show when you're really in trouble?" asks Michael J Bugeja, a professor of communications at Iowa State university of Science and Technology and author of *Interpersonal Divide: The Search for Community in a Technological Age.* He notes the world of difference between someone typing a frowny emoticon upon hearing that you've been in a car crash and showing up to help you get home. He also says that Facebook, with its focus on existing relationships—and its ability to codify and categorize those relationships—in some ways belies the promise of the Internet. "Rather than opening us up to a global community, it is putting us into groups," he says.

That's why Facebook works best as an amplification of a "real life" social life, not a replacement—even as time and technology progress and the lines between online interactions and real-world experiences continue to blur.

SIX

Online Friendships Are Not True Friendships

Eleanor Mills

In the following article Eleanor Mills contends that online friendships are not real friendships. Real friendships, she argues, take a lot of time, energy, and face-to-face contact to cultivate. Online friendships, however, are marked by superficial communication and a show-and-tell nature that makes people feel bad about themselves. She resents social networks giving the impression that friendships can be made by clicking on icons or trading status updates. In her opinion, social networks undermine the social skills necessary to create the kinds of true and lasting friendships that humans need to thrive. Mills concludes that friendships made and maintained over online social networks should not be considered as valuable as in-person friendship.

Mills is a columnist for the *Times*, a London-based newspaper.

Facebook is losing its magic. Last week [May 2010], showing signs of desperation, the social networking site changed its privacy settings in response to an outcry from users over how it was sharing their data with commercial companies.

After spending some time on the site myself, scoping the reactions of Facebookers—the majority of whom slam the company —I'd say it has done too little, too late. Already, the days when

Eleanor Mills, "Facebook's Friendship Trap," *Sunday Times* (London), May 30, 2010, © Times Newspapers Ltd. Reprinted by permission.

you simply *had* to be on Facebook are over; in fact it's cooler now not to be. And revelations about the sordid past of the geeky founder, Mark Zuckerberg (soon to be seen in a film [*The Social Network*, 2010]), aren't helping the firm's image either.

Facebook Does Not Foster True Communication

I've always been a little agnostic about Facebook. I'm on it but in a rather half-hearted way. I'm a passive user; if someone asks to be my friend and I know them, I say yes. But I never go hunting. Occasionally I'll peruse the odd photograph (though I hate it when people put up pics of me). But I find all that constant status-updating irritating.

Do I really want to know that someone I met at a conference is popping out for a coffee? Er . . . no. And the sunlit, airbrushed, smug version of themselves that people promote on the site is frankly tiresome.

Of course, when you're first on it and you realise you can contact pretty well everyone you've ever known, it feels rather exciting. But once you've swapped one of those "Yeah, hi, I'm fine, yes—married, two kids, working as a journalist . . . what about you?" emails with someone you used to go to parties with 20 years ago, that's usually about as far as it goes. Facebook doesn't really put you in touch: after a desultory email or so, communication fizzles out. What the site does do, however, is put all the Facebook-perfect lives of everyone you know within easy reach; and that can be quite a pressure if yours isn't matching up.

Online Networks Undermine Social Skills

Last week my vague feelings of unease about social networking were fanned by a fascinating study by the Mental Health Foundation, which blamed high levels of loneliness among young people on their use of virtual, rather than real, communication. Dubbed the "Eleanor Rigby generation", those aged 18–34 (84% of whom use the internet regularly) are the most likely to be lonely, according to the report. And 31% admitted that they spent too much time online rather than face to face.

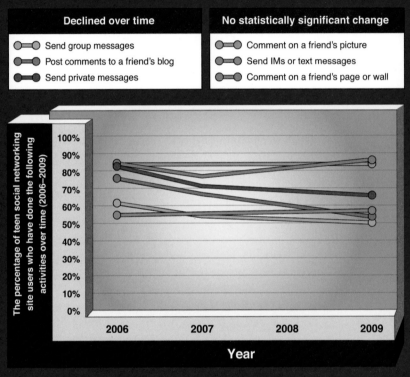

How Teens Use Social Networking Sites

Teens have decreased many of their activities on social networking sites, showing a declining or static interest in using such sites for social purposes.

Declined over time
- Send group messages
- Post comments to a friend's blog
- Send private messages

No statistically significant change
- Comment on a friend's picture
- Send IMs or text messages
- Comment on a friend's page or wall

The percentage of teen social networking site users who have done the following activities over time (2006–2009)

100%
90%
80%
70%
60%
50%
40%
30%
20%
10%
0%

2006   2007   2008   2009

Year

Taken from: Pew Internet & American Life Project, 2009.

The psychologist Dr Aric Sigman says that social networking sites undermine social skills and the ability to read body language. Actual physical contact benefits our wellbeing by boosting levels of the hormone oxytocin. In fact, being lonely is as bad for your health as smoking.

It is not that surprising. After all, human beings are social animals. Our ability to live in groups and co-operate is a key part of our survival as a species. Human beings deprived of others are more prone to anxiety and paranoia. So if you combine physical non-contact—being alone—with a constant stream of information about what a wonderful time all those "friends" are having, you have a classic Petri dish for social anxiety and loneliness.

Friendships Are Not Made by Clicking on Icons

The very language of sites such as Facebook, with its "Would you like to add me as a friend?" lexicon, undermines what real friendship is. I'm not surprised kids are lonely if a whole generation thinks friends can be made by clicking on an icon, and that it's normal to have hundreds of pals. We all know that many of our "friends" are nothing of the sort; the bulk of them are acquaintances or people we hung out with years ago or former colleagues or contacts.

But young people have grown up with social networking, in which your popularity can be easily measured by the number of friends on your Facebook page. They feel under pressure to demonstrate through these sites how busy and social and popular they are. One colleague told me how horrified she was to discover that her quiet, sporty son had posted a photo of himself semi-naked, beer in one hand, girl in the other. "It so wasn't him," she explained. "He was only posting it because peer pressure implies that's what he should be doing. It was probably the only time he'd ever behaved that way."

One of the great curses of modern life is the tyranny of choice. For a young person, particularly, there are so many options, so many possibilities, that it can seem impossible to choose. The corollary of that is a permanent sense of paranoia: that the choice you made was the wrong one, that the party you are at isn't as fun as the other one you could have gone to. That everyone else is more popular or cool, or having more fun. That the grass is always greener somewhere else.

Social networking, with its instant updates and photos, is like rocket fuel to that kind of paranoia. To some of the youngsters I know, it can seem that their whole lives are one long quest for a post or picture to put on their Facebook page to show their peers they're having a really great time. One told me that she'd had a

The author believes that "real" friendships are an antidote to loneliness, soothe the spirit, and balance people's moral compasses.

really terrible night but that it didn't matter because the pics looked great. Hello?

Real Friendships Are Cultivated in Real Life

The secret of happiness is to recognise that, wherever you are, whoever you are with, if you are having fun, then that is the best place to be. Over thousands of years, thinkers have exhorted us to live in the moment, be content with our lot, enjoy where we are.

One of the best bits of growing older is being confident enough to see that right here, right now, is pretty damn good, thanks very much. That the endless search for the coolest party, the hippest club, the most exclusive late-night rave, is a pointless bore. Happiness is being content with where you are and what you've got, not wasting time longing for something else.

The great joy of having a few real friends, rather than hundreds on your Facebook site, is that they love you despite your faults. Crucially, with them, you don't have to put up a front; you can admit that, actually, things aren't that great; that being away from home is hard, that you hate your course, that you behaved like a prat [an idiot].

Real friendships are the antidote to loneliness and the balm of the spirit; they are where we reset our moral compasses, laugh at our idiocies and feel loved and valued for ourselves, not what we pretend to be.

Social networking may be here to stay, but we shouldn't confuse it with the real thing. In an increasingly cyber world, the secret of happiness is probably just getting out there and giving real life a whirl. Who cares what it looks like on Facebook?

SEVEN

Social Networking Can Build Educational Skills

Christina Clark and George Dugdale

Social media can build students' writing and communication skills, argue Christina Clark and George Dugdale in the following viewpoint. They discuss the results of a survey that found that students who have a profile on a social networking site, and/or maintain a blog, write more often than students who neither blog nor participate in social networking. Such students are more likely to enjoy writing and also demonstrate more confidence in their writing. The study found that owning a cell phone, texting, or writing instant messages does not negatively impact a student's writing skills—on the contrary, such endeavors expose them to more writing. Clark and Dugdale conclude that social media can positively impact students' skill in and love of writing and communication.

Clark is head of research at the National Literacy Trust, where Dugdale is a policy adviser.

Writing is an important issue in the UK [United Kingdom] today. While children's and young people's writing standards steadily improved until 2006, levels have not increased in recent years. Writing is much more than just an educational issue—it is an essential skill that allows people to participate fully in today's society and to contribute to the economy.

How Do Today's Students Use Writing?

Previous research into the teaching of writing and effective writing strategies has mainly focused on the formal types of writing taught in schools. However, today's society writing takes many forms, including texting, instant messaging, blogging and emailing. The research evidence about these new forms of writing in the UK is fragmented and inconclusive. In particular, there is a lack of research looking at how much young people write, the different forms of writing that they engage in and their confidence in using these different forms of writing.

Since relatively little is known about young people's views about writing in the UK, the key objectives of this survey were: *to explore how much young people enjoy writing, what type of writing they engage in, how good at writing they think they are and what they think about writing.*

3001 pupils aged 8–16 from England and Scotland completed an online survey in May 2009. There was an almost equal gender split, with 48.6% of boys and 51.4% of girls taking part. The percentage of pupils who receive free school meals (20.2%), which is frequently used in educational research as a crude indicator of socio-economic background, was higher in this survey compared to the national average for primary and secondary pupils.

Social Media Builds Students' Writing Skills

Some of the key findings of this survey are:

75% of young people said that they write regularly. Technology-based formats were most frequently written. For example, 82% of young people wrote text messages at least once a month, 73% wrote instant messages (such as messages on AIM or MSN), and 63% wrote on a social networking site. Of non-technology based writing, 77% wrote notes or answers in class or for homework at least once a month followed by 52% writing notes to other people.

Surveys show that students who have a profile on social networking sites and/or maintain a blog write more than students who do not social network or blog.

[Fifty-six percent] of young people said they had a profile on a social networking site, such as Bebo or Facebook. 24% said that they have their own blog. While frequently vilified in the media as 'dumbing down' young people's literacy, this research shows that technology offers different writing opportunities for young people, which is seen in a link between blogging and (self-reported) writing ability and enjoyment of writing. For example, young people who write on a blog were much more likely than young people who do not write on a blog to enjoy writing in general (57% vs. 40%) and to enjoy writing for family/friends in particular (79% vs. 55%). Young people with a blog (61%) as well as young people with a profile on a social networking site (56%) also displayed greater confidence, believing themselves to be good writers. Blog owners and young people with a social networking profile were also more prolific writers than their counterparts. They held more positive attitudes towards writing and computer use, and viewed writers more favourably.

Computers and Technology Help Students Enjoy Writing

Owning a mobile phone does not appear to alter young people's enjoyment of writing, their writing behaviour or their attitudes towards writing.

Most young people said they used computers regularly and believed that computers are beneficial to their writing, agreeing that a computer makes it easier for them to correct mistakes (89%) and allows them to present ideas clearly (76%). Overall, nearly 60% of young people also believe that computers allow them to be more creative, concentrate more and encourage them to write more often.

Young people are ambivalent about their enjoyment of writing. 45% of young people surveyed said that they enjoy writing. However, enjoyment of writing is related to the type of writing being done. When young people were asked to rate their enjoyment of writing for family/friends and their enjoyment of writing for school separately, some differences emerged. Young people enjoyed writing for family/friends more than they enjoyed writing for school, with over two-thirds of young people enjoying writing for family/friends and only half enjoying writing for schoolwork. Most young people agree that they enjoy writing more when they can choose the topic (79%).

Social Networking and Blogging Boost Writing Skills

A 2009 study found that social network users and blog owners are significantly more likely to write in an array of formats compared with other young people, including notes to other people, short stories, letters, song lyrics, poems, reviews, plays/screenplays, and in a diary/journal.

	Social networking site users %	Non–social networking site users %	Blog owners %	Non-blog owners %
Notes or answers in class/for homework	79.2	76.9	79.3	77.2
Notes to other people	**62.1**	**48.4**	**60.8**	**49.9**
Short stories	**55.3**	**42.1**	**60.1**	**42.9**
Essays	43.0	44.4	43.9	44.0
Letters	**37.8**	**30.1**	**41.4**	**31.2**
Song lyrics	**34.7**	**22.7**	**42.5**	**25.6**
A diary/journal	**34.5**	**23.7**	**44.8**	**24.4**
Reports	32.1	34.7	32.4	33.3
Poems	32.0	32.2	**44.8**	**27.4**
Newspaper or magazine stories	30.6	30.6	34.8	30.3
Reviews	29.1	31.2	**39.6**	**29.8**
Plays/screenplays	28.2	24.0	**34.8**	**24.5**
Postcards	16.0	16.5	16.7	15.9

(Figures in bold indicate that there were statistically significant differences at the conventional significance level of 0.05 between the pairs.)

Taken from: Christina Clark and George Dugdale, "Young People's Writing Attitudes, Behavior and the Role of Technology," National Literacy Trust, November 2009, pp. 19–20.

Troubled Writers Could Benefit from Technology

Echoing US research (Pew Internet, 2008), just under 9 in 10 young people see writing as an important skill to succeed in life, but this means that a sizeable minority (12%) do not consider it an important life skill.

When asked how good they think they are at writing, we found that there was an almost equal split between those who said that they are either very good or good (52%) and those who felt that they could be better or were not very good (45%). Those who responded that they are a 'very good' or 'good' writer were then asked to select from a list the reasons why they think that they are good at writing. Most young people felt that they were a good writer because they use their imagination (39%), know how to type (36%) and spell (33%). By contrast, young people who didn't believe that they were good writers were more likely to emphasise the transcriptional aspects of writing. For example, the most common reason why young people think that they are not good writers is that they are not very good at writing neatly (23%), followed by them not enjoying writing very much (22%), not being very good at spelling (21%) or at checking their work (20%). . . .

Technology Helps Build Writing Skills

In summary, this research provides us with an up-to-date insight into young people's attitudes towards writing. Most young people write regularly and young people write technology-based materials, such as text and instant messages, most frequently. While owning a mobile phone does not appear to alter young people's writing behaviour, having a profile on a social networking site or having a blog is connected to enjoyment of writing and confidence in writing. Young people today use computers regularly and believe that computers are beneficial to their writing.

We believe it is paramount that the school curriculum reflects and utilises writing forms that young people enjoy and engage with, in order to demonstrate that writing is more than a compulsory task: it is an essential life skill.

EIGHT

Facebook Violates Privacy

Bob Sullivan

> Bob Sullivan covers Internet scams and consumer fraud for MSNBC.com. He is also the author of *Gotcha Capitalism: How Hidden Fees Rip You off Every Day and What You Can Do About It.* In the following article he warns that Facebook violates privacy by keeping information posted by users permanently online. Sullivan explains it is very difficult—even impossible—to remove photos, comments, and other classic social networking content from the site. Although a user may not currently care who is privy to this information, Sullivan warns it might someday come back to haunt him should he want to run for public office, apply for a particular type of job, or protect his family from knowing certain things about risky, experimental, or re-grettable periods of his life. Sullivan says most users do not comprehend the threat that social networking poses to their privacy—until it is too late.

I know a computer science professor who runs the same Facebook experiment every semester. He invites his students to stand up in front of the room and show everyone their Facebook page on the big screen. No one has ever taken him up on the offer.

Why? They're embarrassed, of course.

Moments later, the irony sinks in. Every one of them seems happy to share all those funny photographs, witty Wall postings and status updates with everyone on the planet. They just don't want to do it in public, in person.

Facebook puts a lot of people in a lot of twisted situations, including those who try to rationalize their use of the site. (Want to be safer on Facebook? There are tips below).

Studies show that about two-thirds of Americans say they care a great deal about their privacy, yet fewer than 10 percent ever do anything about it, such as destroy a store loyalty card or browse the Web with an anonymizing tool.

So it is with Facebook. This week, a dust-up—no, a tornado —hit the service when users found out about a subtle change to Facebook's terms of service. A blogger at the Consumerist Web site posted the change, noting that Facebook now asserts the right to "copy, publish, store, retain," anything you contribute, and that the firm's rights to your material survive "any termination of your use of the Facebook Service."

In other words, whatever you put on Facebook cannot be deleted. Even closing your account, removing all your pictures, and "de-friending" your friends doesn't get your data back from the Facebook.

Everyone seems shocked by the idea that Facebook is forever, but that's nothing new. In fact, I believe Facebook deserves some kudos for finally fessing up and including this concept in its terms of service. I'm thrilled that people are now discussing this issue.

You Just Can't Kill It

For years, enterprising folks who wanted to delete their Facebook pages found their only real alternative was to "deactivate" their accounts. That's not a subtle distinction. Facebook's terms of service say this: "Individuals who wish to deactivate their Facebook account may do so on the My Account page. Removed information may persist in backup copies for a reasonable period of time but will not be generally available to members of Facebook," it reads.

Obviously, there is a hole so big there that Facebook lawyers could drive a truck through it. And in fact, for years Facebook users who wished to delete their accounts were told they had to manually delete every picture, minifeed item, friend, and so on.

A Facebook user edits his account's privacy settings. Facebook has asserted that it has the right to "copy, publish, store, retain" anything posted to the site, whether or not the user is still using the account.

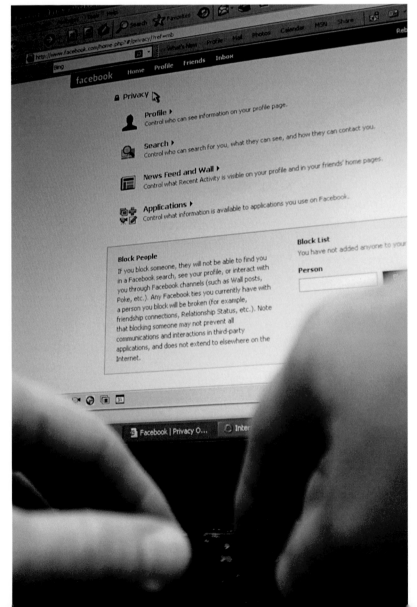

For an hysterical and sad account of this, read "2,504 steps to closing your Facebook account."

Special Series: Privacy Lost

Last year, Facebook tried to address a groundswell of frustration over account deletion and added a process for doing so. Users who follow a link and fill out a form are now told their accounts have been deleted. Even that advance arrived with hiccups, as many who initially tried the process were still able to find their accounts on Google. Facebook said it was a glitch, since fixed. (I'll leave it to readers to consider why Facebook refuses to add a simple "delete my account" button on its site.)

But even after following this deletion process, users might be disappointed. Facebook accounts are so intertwined that traces of deleted members' activities—such as wall posts—can still appear all over the site and remain on Facebook servers indefinitely.

And of course, with some data, there's just no way to remove it:

"Where you make use of the communication features of the service to share information with other individuals on Facebook, however, (e.g., sending a personal message to another Facebook user) you generally cannot remove such communications," the Facebook terms of service agreement reads.

This should give pause to any Facebook user who plans to get a job or have children some day. Heaven forbid you decide to run for Congress 20 years from now. And we haven't even mentioned Facebook's Beacon disaster, which saw the company introduce an advertising platform that followed users around the Web and reported their behavior to friends. Facebook quickly backtracked after a similar uproar.

Facebook and Privacy Don't Mix

By now, it should be clear that I'm a Facebook hater. I think there is no way to use the site and maintain control of your privacy. In fact, I think there is essentially no way to stay off Facebook now, which offends my sensibilities. More than once I've arrived at

"This is so sudden. I never had a chance to check you out on Facebook, Google, and MySpace."

"This is so sudden." cartoon by Aaron Bacall. www.CartoonStock.com.

work and had someone say something like this: "Hey, I saw you were at Murphy's last night," because someone I barely know posted a bunch of pictures of a happy hour. That's spooky.

I have a friend who is a foreign diplomat; she takes rather Draconian steps to prevent such a Facebook oops from occurring. At the end of every party, she walks around, grabs everyone's camera, and deletes any pictures of herself.

I know many of you believe that you have nothing to hide, and the idea that your children might some day see your Facebook page doesn't (currently) bother you at all. But here's the problem with any privacy-related choice: it's usually impossible to assess tomorrow's consequences today. Or, to be blunt, you just never know what might come back and bite you in the butt.

What if employment background companies someday discover that anyone with more than 500 Facebook friends tends to come in late to work? No, there's nothing illegal about that. What if you change career paths at some point and decide you want to work for a U.S. intelligence agency? You'll have to answer for every foreign friend linked to you on Facebook—and any who ever were linked to you on Facebook.

As a general rule, you should never put anything on your Facebook account that you wouldn't mind showing to a room full of co-workers or students.

If You Must Facebook, Follow These Rules

That said, the company has quietly been improving its privacy controls and now does offer users a wide set of tools to protect them from each other. There is a long list of options on Facebook's settings pages—probably far more than you're aware of—that users should deploy when using the site. These prevent perfect strangers from knowing you've left your girlfriend and can also prevent your boss from seeing pictures of last week's happy hour.

These options are elegantly summarized in a post on AllFacebook.com written by Nick O'Neill. No one should use Facebook without adjusting these settings. These include removing yourself from Google searches, using friend lists to control who sees your pictures, and how to keep your friendships private.

If all this appropriately spooks you, you can delete your account by following this link.

Interestingly, when you visit it, you'll be presented with this surprising plea for reconsideration.

"Are you deleting because you are concerned about Facebook's Terms of Service? This was a mistake that we have now corrected," the page says before asking users for their e-mail address and password.

Breaking up is hard to do, it seems. Alas, in life, nothing lasts forever. Except on Facebook—and on the Internet—where everything lasts forever.

NINE

It Is Unreasonable to Expect Privacy When Using Facebook

Ben Parr

In the following viewpoint Ben Parr argues that social networking and privacy do not naturally go hand in hand. Parr says Facebook is designed to share, rather than protect, information. The very idea that there can be privacy in social networking is, in his opinion, a contradiction. Parr says if people want privacy, they should not post information online. He says it is up to Facebook users to protect their own privacy. Parr concludes that social networks have changed the nature of privacy and users must realize they are responsible for guarding their personal information.

Parr writes a weekly social media column called "The Social Analyst" that is published on Mashable.com, of which he is coeditor.

All eyes are on Facebook. Ever since Facebook revealed Facebook Open Graph,[1] the world's largest social network has been getting hammered by tech pundits, mainstream media and its users.

Facebook's used to this type of uproar after it changes something, but in my time tracking Facebook, I've never seen anything like this. Not even the Facebook News Feed fiasco of 2006 had

1. A platform that allows people to interact with certain features of Facebook without logging into the site.

U.S. Senate scrutiny. Facebook Open Graph has clearly struck a nerve with a lot of people.

Is Facebook betraying its users, though? Has Facebook compromised user privacy? After taking a lot of time to absorb the arguments and the big picture, I'm weighing in, and I doubt that my conclusion is going to be popular.

The central problem is that people believe that Facebook and the web in general should be able to protect the information we post online. I argue that this is untrue, because it goes against the fundamental design of Facebook, social media, and the web itself. We should be relying on ourselves for our privacy, and not turning Facebook into our convenient scapegoat. . . .

Social Networks Are Designed to Share, Not Protect

In 2006, while I was still a junior at Northwestern University, I started a group called Students Against Facebook News Feed. It was the largest protest group against News Feed, which had recently launched at the time. My concern was privacy: I thought that Facebook was violating my privacy and not giving me enough options to control it. 750,000+ other Facebook users agreed—nearly 10% of the user base at the time.

Facebook appeased us with more privacy controls, but they didn't take down News Feed. It has turned out to be the right decision. News Feed has become a central pillar of Facebook and indeed of all social media. Here's what I said about News Feed, two years after the controversy:

> Here's the major change in the last two years: We are more comfortable sharing our lives and thoughts instantly to thousands of people, close friends and strangers alike. The development of new technology and the rocking of the boat by [Facebook founder Mark] Zuckerberg has led to this change.

I actually agree with Mark: Privacy is dead, and social media is holding the smoking gun. Facebook, social media, and even the web itself are designed to share information. While you can be (justifiably) angry about Facebook's lack of communication over the privacy issue, to believe that information on Facebook or other social networks is inherently private or "yours" is just wrong.

I don't care if you have taken every precaution to keep your information private to just a few people: all it takes is one friend copying and pasting that information and posting it somewhere else to "breach" the privacy wall.

The truth is that the privacy wall didn't exist in the first place. The web makes the transmission of information easier than ever. Social media makes spreading that information an even simpler task. An embarrassing picture can go from Facebook upload to public blog post in a matter of minutes. Even if you don't participate in any type of social media, someone can still take what they know about you and put it online.

Protecting Our Privacy Is Up to Us, Not Facebook

The web is now the world's social platform, and expecting any privacy controls or security settings to protect us is just irresponsible. Facebook's not the enemy: it's just the latest scapegoat for our fears and concerns surrounding the new world in which we live.

Before the web, if you wanted to keep something private, you didn't talk about it. It was easier to track whether or not someone was spilling your secrets because you didn't have as many suspects. That's not true if you post information online, though. What was once gossip is now a "privacy leak."

Why do we still expect anything to stay private in the YouTube and Facebook world? More and more, our habit is to share the pictures we take on our camera phones on Facebook, to share what we say over Twitter, and to upload the videos we record on our Flips. Almost everything is being caught by some form of social media these days.

Protecting our privacy starts with us, not Facebook. While the company should have more clearly communicated its recent privacy changes, if you didn't want your pictures shared with the rest of the world, you shouldn't upload them in the first place.

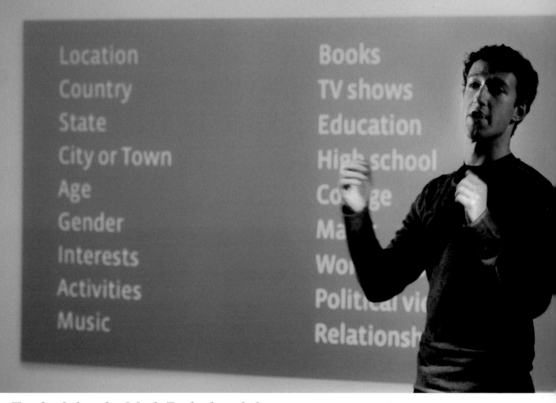

Facebook founder Mark Zuckerberg believes users are comfortable sharing their lives and thoughts instantly. Many people say Facebook's News Feed feature is invasive of privacy.

If You Want Something Kept Private, Do Not Post It

Actually, in the social media world, you shouldn't be placing yourself in positions where people can take embarrassing photos of you. Yes, it's unfortunate that the dumb mistakes teenagers make are getting posted online for the world to see, but that's how the world works now.

What Happens Online Stays Online

A 2009 survey by CareerBuilder found that 45 percent of employers use social networking sites to research potential employees, and 11 percent plan to start doing so. Furthermore, 35 percent said they found content on social networking sites that caused them not to hire someone. Among these reasons were the following:

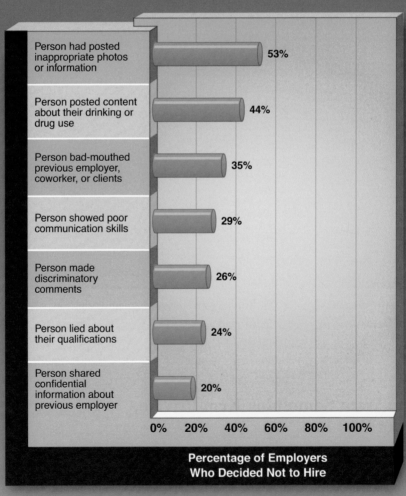

Person had posted inappropriate photos or information	53%
Person posted content about their drinking or drug use	44%
Person bad-mouthed previous employer, coworker, or clients	35%
Person showed poor communication skills	29%
Person made discriminatory comments	26%
Person lied about their qualifications	24%
Person shared confidential information about previous employer	20%

0%   20%   40%   60%   80%   100%

**Percentage of Employers
Who Decided Not to Hire**

Taken from: Careerbuilder.com, August 19, 2009.

Facebook isn't to blame for how the web has changed our world. They are just embracing emerging trends and making the web more efficient in their wake. Being able to broadcast what I like on the web to all of my friends is smart, and making it easy for me to do that (via "Like" buttons) is brilliant.

I defend Facebook's ambitious Open Graph project, because it does make the browsing experience better: syncing the interests I've posted to the website I visit is a natural extension of the Facebook platform, not a coldly-calculated invasion of my privacy. It will prove to be an innovation that makes the web more useful and more social.

Facebook Is the Wrong Target for Our Anger

I think what I said [in 2009] about social media, Facebook News Feed, and privacy still sums up my feelings best, so I want to quote my past self one more time:

> The thing we've realized is that we still have control over our privacy. It's called choice. If you're uncomfortable with speaking to people digitally, you can decline to sign up for those social media websites. Or you update them differently than others. I can either block relationship updates from News Feed or, in my case, I just never update about it.
>
> News Feed truly launched a revolution that requires us to stand back to appreciate. Privacy has not disappeared, but become even easier to control—what I want to share, I can share with everyone. What I want to keep private stays in my head.
>
> All of this in just two years. Just imagine how social media will change our society in two more.
>
> I look forward to sharing my life and my experience with even more people. I'm not afraid of losing my privacy anymore. You shouldn't be, either.

I defend Facebook because it is the wrong target for our anger. It has done more to bring people together than any technology of the last five years, and the good it has brought far outweighs the bad. We made the decision to turn our personal information over to a private company, and for the most part Facebook made good use of it.

Quitting Facebook won't solve the privacy conundrum: common sense and better education about how privacy has changed will. This debate has once again exposed the gap between how the world has changed and our assumptions about how the world works or should work. Attacking Facebook won't help us come to terms with our society's struggle over the changing nature of privacy.

TEN

Citizen Journalists Threaten the Quality of Journalism

Frédéric Filloux

Frédéric Filloux is a Paris-based writer and media consultant. In the following article he argues that citizen journalism threatens the quality and craft of journalism. Filloux explains that citizen journalists are untrained civilians who report goings on via social networks like Twitter or by filing comments or first-person stories on websites. In Filloux's opinion, these stories are unedited, biased, and prone to error. Real journalists, he says, are trained to painstakingly check their work, properly interview people, present a balanced view of the story, and vet their sources. He disagrees with the idea that anyone can be a journalist—journalism is a professional craft that requires years of training, he says. Filloux warns that the tide of citizen journalism is bad for news and bad for democracy. Just as he would not trust a "citizen surgeon" or a "citizen accountant," so too Filloux says citizen journalists should not be trusted to deliver quality news.

L et's fire a few missiles at politically correct ideas such as "Digital media makes all of us journalists," "citizens will soon displace professional reporters," and so on. That's nonsense (I have more explicit words in mind). Does it mean public input in news should be kept at bay? Certainly not. Quite the contrary, actually. Newsrooms have a challenge on their hands, they need to get better at handling such input.

Never Trust Amateurs with a Professional Job

First, would you trust a citizen neurosurgeon to remove your kid's neuroblastoma? No, you wouldn't. You would not trust a citizen dentist either for your cavities. Or even a people's car repairman. Then, for information, why in hell would we accept practices we wouldn't even contemplate for our health (OK, big issue), or for our washing machine?

Fact is, with the advent of digital media, the very notion of rigor and accuracy has become more . . . fuzzy, more analog. As I said here many times, we are now facing three types of news: the *Commodity* one (everyone gets the same account of the oil spill in Louisiana or the deadly unrest in Thailand); *Mashup* news (the more it buzzes, the better it works); and the *Quality Niche*, that tries to defend its standards. The first two are expanding and the third is getting to look like a Zant currant [very small seedless black grape], (*Raisin sec* in French): good, tasty, but tiny and dry. And produced in small quantities.

Journalism Is a Painstaking Craft

A couple of weeks ago, a friend of mine sent me a remarkable piece about fact checking at the *New Yorker*. In a loving and witty rendition, the author, John McPhee, details how an army of minutiae-obsessed researchers will spend days to check the smallest assertions in order to remove even the palest shadow of doubt. . . .

A few years back, this colleague showed me a mail exchange he had with a sub-editor at a major US daily about a long feature story of his. Its original submission triggered a long email with dozens of questions about every aspect of the story: "Who says this? Could you add a source of this data? Isn't there a contradiction between this figure and the other in paragraph six? Can you be more specific on this and that?" It went on and on. The story was actually seen as a good one; the painstaking editing, checking and challenging process was merely standard procedure.

Who has the luxury of applying such treatment to news material, nowadays? No one, almost. Only some "Zant currant" news organizations are still holding firm on such a practice. Which leads us to my point: journalism is a profession; it comes with standards, techniques, and a certain level of demand, from the author and his/her editors. . . .

A blogger reports from the Democratic National Convention. Bloggers have been criticized for submitting unedited stories containing biases and errors.

The Medium May Change, but News Needs to Be Delivered by Journalists

In this context, *Blogs* range from the best to the worst. Professional blogs—either independent or hosted by traditional medias—can be the most advanced form of written journalism. Quite often, blogs produced by good journalists are as insightful as standard stories, but way more fun to read. (In France, I do know editors who wish their writers were as witty in the paper as they are on their blogs). Good bloggers sometimes border on columnists. Their work is solid, precise and, sometimes, edited; they take time to write their pieces and it shows.

At the other end of the spectrum, blogs can be utterly superficial, lacking precise facts, or agenda-driven and written with a shovel. Unfortunately, both kinds of blogs are sometimes found under the same roof. In many news organizations, big and small, instead of being considered as a more modern form of journalism, the "blog" name tag is a synonym for lower expectations.

The same kind of carelessness goes for comments. I do believe that opening news content to public feedback is a good thing. At its very core, journalism begs for argument; pundits need detractors. But most online editors satisfy themselves by opening the floodgate of comments, without a strategy, or even the slightest attention to content. As a result, everybody loses: the writer who sees painstaking work defaced by shouts; and the publication for allowing substandard, unmoderated feedback. Participation without relevancy is pointless. Unfortunately, in most news sites— including big ones, very little thought seems to have been given to raising the level of public contributions.

Untrained Citizens Cannot Produce Quality Journalism

This leads us to the oxymoronic notion of citizen journalism. Using public contributions to compensate for the absence of a reporter on the scene is nothing new. For decades, finding pictures taken by witnesses (sometimes paying for such) has been part of the job. Today, Twitter has replaced the checkbook. In many instances, Twitter has proven extraordinary precious and efficient. But, soon, the spontaneous stream of accounts has to be supplemented by professional editing and checking. This is the kind of powerful combination that made the coverage of civil unrests in Tibet or Iran so compelling.

Last March [2009], professor George Brock, head of journalism at the City University of London, gave an absolute must-read lecture on the evolution of journalism titled "Is 'News' Over?" Here is what he said about readers' input:

> This is a competition for trust between two different forms of collective intelligence. This argument is not being openly and clearly mapped by those who run news media. Perhaps understandably, no editor wanting to encourage the highest level of participation online wants to underline that the suggestions, tweets, tips and facts flowing in from this rich new sources are being filtered in a traditional way. But the facts of news consumption on the web

tell us clearly that filtering is exactly what people tend to prefer when they have the choice. Filtering used in the old days to be known as "editing." If it's done right, it should be for the benefit and protection of the viewer or reader. It should create trust.

Journalism Requires Skill and Precision

These distinctions are essential to the preservation of quality journalism. Many wondered why the Yahoos, Googles, Microsofts, were unable to set up news organizations despite their incommensurable wealth (to put things in perspective: Google spends five times more each year for its datacenters than the *New York Times* spends for its entire newsroom). Part of the reason is the return on such an investment. Financially speaking, the news business is not very appealing. . . .

But, to thrive, journalism requires more than a checkbook. It has to be built around a set of cultural traits that are in total contradiction to the engineering efficiencies of a search engine or an internet portal. Evidently, the modern news business requires more technology; and journalists need the dialectics from their public. But news requires more professionalism than mere crowd-powered demagoguery. Today and, I believe, for as long as trust is to be part of the relationship with readers.

ELEVEN

Citizen Journalists Improve Journalism

Jason Stverak

In the following viewpoint Jason Stverak argues that citizen journalists play a critical role in delivering today's news. He explains that as more newspapers have become unprofitable, they have had to let staff go, leaving a shortage of news professionals. Someone has to provide the news in the wake of this absence, and citizen journalists are successfully filling this gap, he says. Citizen journalists have broken critical investigative stories, including those involving misused government funds, mismanaged equipment, and important lifestyle trends. Stverak concludes that citizen journalists have much to offer the changing face of the news business and their contribution should not be overlooked by traditional media.

Stverak is president of the Franklin Center for Government and Public Integrity, a nonprofit organization that provides reporters, citizens, and nonprofit organizations with training, expertise, and support.

Traditional news media reporters and editors are being devastated by a financial crisis, not a journalism crisis. Somebody has to fill the void.

The Future of Citizen Journalism

According to a 2007 We Media–Zogby online poll, Americans are dissatisfied with the quality of American journalism today, and as a result, many believe citizen journalists, bloggers, and other emerging figures can play a positive role in America's news delivery system.

The Role of Citizen Journalism

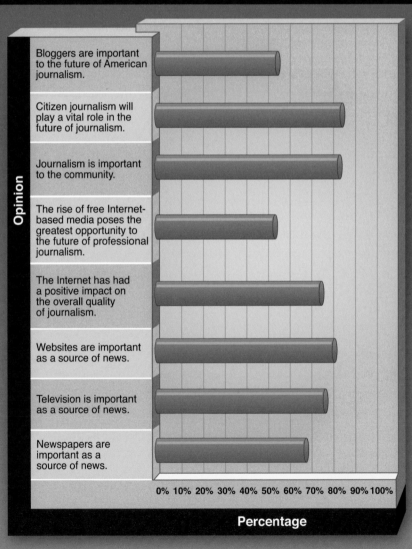

Opinion

- Bloggers are important to the future of American journalism.
- Citizen journalism will play a vital role in the future of journalism.
- Journalism is important to the community.
- The rise of free Internet-based media poses the greatest opportunity to the future of professional journalism.
- The Internet has had a positive impact on the overall quality of journalism.
- Websites are important as a source of news.
- Television is important as a source of news.
- Newspapers are important as a source of news.

0% 10% 20% 30% 40% 50% 60% 70% 80% 90% 100%

Percentage

Taken from: We Media–Zogby Poll, February 2007.

Those of us who work with citizen journalists in online news ventures know better than anyone what a tough, disciplined calling it is. That is why we hire professionals and rigorously train citizens.

We also know the future is online. And online news produced by citizen journalists can toss traditional media the lifeline they so desperately need.

Decentralizing the News Makes It Available to All

Face facts: Traditional media have put journalism last for at least a decade, cutting thousands of jobs and wondering why readers, viewers and listeners flee. America lost a generation of professional journalists. That is a serious threat to self-government. How will we replace them?

Reanimation of journalism arises in online news ventures. The blogosphere is no longer just for the ranters and ideologues. Increasingly, straight-shooting journalists cut from newsrooms join online non-profit ventures. There they get the opportunity to reemerge as hard-news reporters of yesteryear who investigate stories traditional media now cannot or will not cover.

By decentralizing the news business, investigative reporters for online non-profits are creating quality coverage of America's most important issues and making it available to all.

Someone Has to Fill the Void

The rise of online non-profit investigative journalism stems not only from the overall newsroom cuts around the nation, but also from the growing vacuum in state-based coverage. Many traditional newsrooms no longer have the staff or financial resources to send a reporter across town, let alone cross-country, to investigate a story.

For at least a decade, newspapers have curbed reporters' ability to investigate major stories while producing daily beat copy to feed the beast. With the accelerating decline of professional investigative journalists at state-wide newspapers and television stations, how is corruption supposed to be exposed? Who is scrutinizing the mountain of public records and attending meetings? Who is developing sources and asking tough questions to expose fraud, corruption and waste?

Citizen Journalists Have Broken Critical Stories

Just recently, a series of state-based watchdog groups proved online news websites can churn out investigative pieces and breaking news stories. The effects of their reporting has impacted the entire nation.

- An online journalist broke the "Phantom Congressional District" story about the chaos in tracking American Recovery and Reinvestment Act funds. On November 16, 2009, Jim Scarantino, the investigative reporter for New Mexico's Rio Grande Foundation, discovered that the Recovery.gov website listing federal stimulus money was riddled with ludicrous errors. His online story prompted other citizen journalists he had networked with through the Franklin Center for Government and Public Integrity to look into their own state's recovery.gov data. When all was said and done, these online journalists found that $6.4 billion in stimulus funds had been awarded to 440 non-existent Congressional districts in all 50 states, the District of Columbia, and four American territories.
- It was an online journalist in New Hampshire who broke the news when [former House Speaker] Newt Gingrich admitted during an interview he made an endorsement mistake in a highly contested congressional race.
- A Watchdog in Texas recently discovered that the Department of Homeland Security lost nearly 1,000 computers in 2008.
- An online reporter in Minnesota got the attention of the state government when his organization, the Freedom Foundation of Minnesota, released a report proving that Minnesotans were leaving the state due to high taxes.
- And it was a reporter in Hawaii who delved into House Speaker Nancy Pelosi's pricey holiday trip, which included an astonishing $10,000 nightly expense and more than $21,000 in security cost to Hawaii's taxpayers.

In addition to quality news coverage, many of these non-profit online news organizations offer a "steal our stuff" policy that provides newspapers with free news. This is an obvious cost advantage over the traditional news wires that charge for content.

Do Not Discount What Citizen Journalists Have to Offer

As more non-profit journalism organizations develop, and more online journalists emerge in cities around the nation, the traditional wire services will have stiff competition unless they deal with reality and start picking up the best work these journalists produce. Non-profit journalism organizations as well as citizen

Bloggers attend a conference in Nashville, Tennessee, to train in techniques used by mainstream journalists. The author claims bloggers have made significant contributions to the news industry.

journalists are producing news that too often is overlooked by traditional media. Not all those who write online stories are journalists —yet—but the ones who are should get the same access and treatment as those few still employed by newspapers, television and radio.

At the end of the day, a partnership between newspapers and citizen journalism organizations will be beneficial not only for both, but also for Americans who will be better informed. That's the point. It also is the mission.

TWELVE

Social Networking Can Facilitate Democracy and Peace in Other Countries

Kathleen Parker

Kathleen Parker is a columnist for the *Washington Post*. In the following viewpoint she argues that social networking can facilitate worldwide peace. She discusses the Israeli-Palestinian conflict, a decades-old struggle that has yet to be resolved. Parker suggests that social media and online networks might play a role in solving such conflicts. She explains that communication is key to supporting peace and preventing war, and social networks are excellent vehicles for connecting people and fostering communication. Social networks also expose users to people living outside their communities, which helps them learn about and better tolerate different cultures. Parker thinks that if everyone added someone from an enemy country to his or her Facebook page, it would be a good way to start working toward a more peaceful and tolerant world.

As Israeli and Palestinian leaders reopen Mideast peace negotiations, a phrase that computers worldwide autocomplete from habit of repetition, Planet Earth rolls her eyes. Been there, done that, gave away the T-shirt decades ago.

Social networking was a unifying force that helped organize peaceful protests against Egypt's president Hosni Mubarak in January 2011.

Can anyone really hope that this time—This Time!—things will be different?

But. There may be hope yet, if not this moment, then in the near future, thanks to other factors possibly not considered. To illustrate, two scenarios:

At the State Department, Secretary of State Hillary Clinton sits between Israeli Prime Minister Binyamin Netanyahu and Palestinian Authority President Mahmoud Abbas. There is much gray hair among them.

Not far away, at a sidewalk cafe near George Washington University, four college students converse amicably. One is Israeli, one Palestinian, another Syrian, the fourth African American. (One of my young tablemates knows and identifies them.) Their iPhones join flatware among platters of couscous and falafel. They are speaking English, laughing, trading news and barbs.

The scene just described is not rare in the nation's capital or in many other cities where colleges and universities attract diverse populations. I've witnessed variations of the same tableau dozens of times. Different faces, ethnicities and nationalities, but the same dynamic and, for members of an older generation, the same revelation.

The ancient rivalries and the heavy burden of history are being lifted among a rising generation of world citizens even as the taupe generation rehashes the same—may I just say—absurd arguments over who gets to claim which square inch of the sandbox.

That is so last millennium.

Enter the Facebook generation, for whom el mundo es un pañuelo, as perhaps 500 million people might put it. Translation: It's a small world. When one can communicate with another with a keystroke or a click, the world is a computer bit.

As I watched these four interact, it occurred to me that in Facebook world, where friends connect, and friends of friends "friend" each other, and networks of associations expand like a circulatory system to all reaches permitted by technology (and governments), it is increasingly unlikely that warring factions can sustain themselves for much longer in the grand scheme of things. Friends don't kill friends—most of the time.

We seem to understand the opportunities social networking provides for commercial and political purposes. Barack Obama is president in no small part because of the grass-roots facility of social media. That same power can be harnessed for peace. In fact, it is happening under our noses.

But why not be strategic about something so easily channeled for good?

In a virtual universe, where Google can translate almost any language instantaneously, younger people of all nationalities are creating and communicating through a common idiom.

Not to be a Pollyanna, but it is striking to realize that peace becomes plausible when barriers to communication are eliminated. More than 500 million people use Facebook alone. Of those,

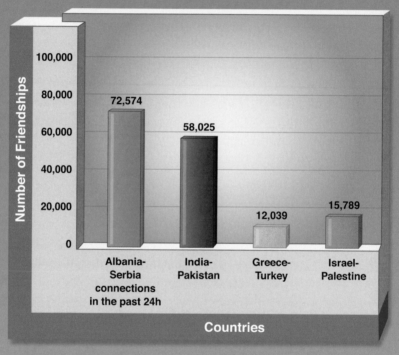

Global Friendships on Facebook

Each day people of different countries, religions, and political affiliations connect on Facebook. This graph captures connections made during a twenty-four-hour span in October 2010.

Below are the friend connections created each day between people of different countries, religions, and political affiliations.

Number of Friendships

100,000	
80,000	72,574
60,000	58,025
40,000	
20,000	12,039 15,789
0	

Albania-Serbia connections in the past 24h — India-Pakistan — Greece-Turkey — Israel-Palestine

Countries

Taken from: Peace on Facebook, www.peace.facebook.com, October 25, 2010.

70 percent are outside the United States. MySpace has 122 million monthly active users, and Twitter reports 145 million registered users.

Obviously, some countries don't like these media for the very reasons we do. People talk. Facebook is blocked in Syria and China and until recently was also blocked in Iran, Pakistan and Bangladesh. Where freedom flourishes, so do open channels of communication.

And vice versa.

We also know that where freedom and communication thrive, wars are less likely. This isn't computer science but human nature. Hence, we gather around heavy tables to talk things out.

Meanwhile, evidence mounts that sentiments are shifting among younger people, whose worldviews are broader than those of previous generations. Recent polling by Frank Luntz found that American Jewish college students are more willing than their elders to question the Israeli position. They resist groupthink and desperately want peace.

Might Palestinian youth feel similarly? Alas, I could find no similar polls.

If I were dictator for a day, I would arrange for every young person to "friend" another in the enemy camp of their choice, creating virtual student-exchange programs in every neighborhood on the map. While the old folks bicker over their sandboxes, the children could begin building fortresses of friendship.

THIRTEEN

Social Networking Cannot Facilitate Democracy and Peace in Other Countries

Evgeny Morozov

In the following article Evgeny Morozov argues that social media will not necessarily encourage peace and democracy in other countries. He says it is too easy to think that just giving oppressed peoples Facebook, Twitter, and Wiki technology will let them connect with each other and rise up against their dictators. In reality, says Morozov, such social media can actually inhibit participation in politics because unlike real-life protest movements, social media has no central organizing body or top-down hierarchical revolutionary structure. Furthermore, Morozov points out that in Western countries, social media is largely used for social and silly ends. He thinks it is hypocritical to expect that oppressed peoples would find a more noble use for it. Finally, Morozov says that even if oppressed peoples were to use social media to organize and protest, so too could their oppressors. He explains that terrorists and dictatorships have already used the Internet to organize and further their oppression. For these reasons, Morozov says it is unrealistic to think that social media can play a significant role in democracy, peace, and freedom movements.

Morozov is the author of *The Net Delusion: The Dark Side of Internet Freedom*. He is also a contributing editor to *Foreign Policy* and runs the magazine's *Net Effect* blog about the Internet's impact on global politics.

A storm of protest hit Google last week over Buzz, its new social networking service, because of user concerns about the inadvertent exposure of their data. Internet users in Iran, however, were spared such trouble. It's not because Google took extra care in protecting their identities—they didn't—but because the Iranian authorities decided to ban Gmail, Google's popular email service, and replace it with a national email stystem that would be run by the government.

Such paradoxes abound in the Islamic Republic's complex relationship with the Internet. As the Iranian police were cracking down on anti-government protesters by posting their photos online and soliciting tips from the public about their identities, a technology company linked to the government was launching the first online supermarket in the country. Ony a few days later, Iran's state-controlled telecommunications company confirmed it had struck an important deal with its peers in Azerbaijan and Russia, boosting the country's communications capacity and lessening its dependence on Internet cables that pass through the United Arab Emirates and Turkey.

Most of these paradoxes are lost on Western observers of the Internet and its role in the politics of Iran and other authoritarian states. Since the publication of John Perry Barlow's "Declaration of the Independence of Cyberspace" in 1996, they have been led to believe that cyberspace is conducive to democracy and liberty, and no government would be able to crush that libertarian spirit (why, then, Mr. Barlow felt the need to write such a declaration remains unknown to this day). The belief that free and unfettered access to information, combined with new tools of mobilization afforded by blogs and social networks, leads to the opening up of authoritarian societies and their eventual democratization now forms one of the pillars of "techno-utopianism."

Secretary of State Hillary Clinton vows to make Internet freedom one of the cornerstones of American foreign policy, and one senator after another issues calls to "tear down this cyber wall" and allocate more funding to groups that promote Internet freedom and fight online censorship without giving much thought to the footnotes. The spirit of techno-utopianism in Washington rides so high it often seems that the Freedom Agenda has been reborn as the Twitter Agenda—perhaps only with more utopianism about both democratization and the Internet's role in it. Even such a seasoned observer of foreign affairs as Republican Sen. Richard Lugar of Indiana could not resist the urge to join the church of Twitter-worship, penning a Foreign Policy op-ed that urged American diplomats to engage with social media. What remains overlooked by Sen. Lugar and others is that authoritarian governments may survive the age of information abundance relatively unscathed —and in fact, they're already using the Internet to fight the challenges posed by modernity.

Is this growing fascination with social media a mere sign of our desperation with other, more conventional instruments of diplomatic leverage? Perhaps so. While sanctions and negotiations —the well-tested ways of wielding American power—do not get us very far with China and Iran, social media as a tool of foreign policy has the unique advantage of being untested. It never failed—so it must be working.

It's easy to see why a world in which young Iranians embrace the latest technology funded by venture capitalists from Silicon Valley, while American diplomats sit back, sip tea and shovel the winter snow on a break from work, sounds so appealing. But is such a world achievable? Will Twitter and Facebook come to the rescue and fill in the void left by more conventional tools of diplomacy? Will the oppressed masses in authoritarian states join the barricades once they get unfettered access to Wikipedia and Twitter?

This seems quite unlikely. In fact, our debate about the Internet's role in democratization—increasingly dominated by techno-utopianism—is in dire need of moderation, for there are at least as many reasons to be skeptical. Ironically, the role that the Internet played in the recent events in Iran shows us why:

Iranian bloggers work at an Internet café in Tehran. The author believes Iran's Green Movement, a protest group, has been compromised by government actions to spread pro-government propaganda on the Internet.

Revolutionary change that can topple strong authoritarian regimes requires a high degree of centralization among their opponents. The Internet does not always help here. One can have "organizing without organizations"—the phrase is in the subtitle of "Here Comes Everybody," Clay Shirky's bestselling 2008 book about the power of social media—but one can't have revolutions without revolutionaries.

Contrary to the utopian rhetoric of social media enthusiasts, the Internet often makes the jump from deliberation to participation even more difficult, thwarting collective action under the heavy pressure of never-ending internal debate. This is what may explain the impotence of recent protests in Iran: Thanks to the sociability and high degree of decentralization afforded by the Internet, Iran's Green Movement has been split into so many competing debate chambers—some of them composed primarily of net-savvy Iranians in the diaspora—that it couldn't collect itself on the eve of the 31st anniversary of the Islamic revolution. The Green Movement may have simply drowned in its own tweets.

The government did its share to obstruct its opponents, too. Not only did it thwart Internet communications, the government (or its plentiful loyalists) also flooded Iranian Web sites with videos of dubious authenticity—one showing a group of protesters burning the portrait of Ali Khamenei—that aimed to provoke and splinter the opposition. In an environment like this—where it's impossible to distinguish whether your online interlocutors are your next-door neighbors, some hyperactive Iranians in the diaspora, or a government agent masquerading as a member of the Green Movement—who could blame ordinary Iranians for not taking the risks of flooding the streets only to find themselves arrested?

Our earlier, unfounded expectations that the Internet would make it easy for the average citizens to see who else is opposing the regime and then act collectively based on that shared knowledge may have been inaccurate. In the age of the Spinternet, when cheap online propaganda can easily be bought with the help of pro-government bloggers, elucidating what fellow citizens think about the regime may be harder than we thought. Add to that the growing surveillance capacity of modern authoritarian states—also greatly boosted by information collected through social media and analyzed with new and advanced forms of data-mining—and you may begin to understand why the Green Movement faltered.

The excessive attention that many Western observers devoted to the role of the Internet in the Iranian protests also reveals another, more serious impact that techno-utopianism has on how we think about the Internet in an authoritarian context. Unable to transcend the hackneyed framework of post-electoral protest, we are becoming blind to more general changes and effects that the Internet has on authoritarian societies in between elections. We spend so much time thinking about the dissidents and how the Internet has changed their lives, that we have almost completely neglected how it affects the lives of the average, non-politicized users, who would be crucial to any democratic revolution.

For example, while the American public is actively engaged in a rich and provocative debate about the Internet's impact on our own society—asking how new technologies affect our privacy or how they change the way we read and think—we gloss over such subtleties when talking about the Internet's role in authoritarian countries. It's hard to imagine a mainstream American magazine running a cover story entitled "Is Google Making Us Stupid? The Case of China," as the Atlantic did (without the China part) in 2008. Such attitudes almost smack of orientalism-in-reverse: While we fret about the Internet's contribution to degrading the civic engagement of American kids, all teenagers in China or Iran are presumed to be committed and engaged global citizens who use the Web to acquaint themselves with human rights violations committed by their governments.

This is not to say that there are no young people living under authoritarian conditions who have used the Internet to organize a protest; they exist and should be applauded for their courage. But we should not lose sight of the fact that they are only a tiny minority. For the vast majority of Internet users in those countries, increased access to information by itself may not always be liberating. In fact, it may only undermine their commitment to political dissent.

The case of East Germany offers some valuable lessons here. According to data compiled by the East German government, East Germans who watched West German television were paradoxically more satisfied with life in their country and the communist regime. Speaking in 1990, the East German writer Christoph Hein spoke of the difficulties of mobilizing his fellow citizens, pointing out that "the whole people could leave the country and move to the West . . . at 8 p.m.—via television." Ironically, the fact that Dresden—where the 1989 protests started—lies too far and too low to have received Western broadcasts may partly explain the rebellious spirit of the city's inhabitants.

The parallels to the Internet with its endless supply of online entertainment are obvious: Twitter and Facebook might make political mobilization of the kind that is required to topple dictators harder, not easier.

Our binary view of modern authoritarianism as an endless struggle between the state and its anti-state, pro-Western and pro-democratic opponents also blinds us to the fact that public life in these societies has many more layers and textures. Not all opponents of the Russian or Chinese or even Egyptian state fit the neoliberal pattern. Nationalism, extremism and religious fanaticism abound; Hezbollah and the Muslim Brotherhood are very active online too. It's not at all guaranteed that empowering those forces by weakening the state with the help of the Internet is going to speed up the process of democratization.

Facebook and Twitter empower all groups—not just the pro-Western groups that we like. To put it in a more formal framework: not all social capital created by the Internet is bound to produce "social goods"; "social bads" are inevitable as well. The political scientist Robert Putnam, who was instrumental in promoting the notion of "social capital" in popular discourse, was not blind to such possibilities. In "Bowling Alone," his most famous book, he explicitly cautioned against the "kumbaya interpretation of social capital," stating that "networks . . . are generally good for those inside the network, but the external effects of social capital are by no means always positive."

Thus, it's not just the women's movement that is using Facebook to promote its causes in Saudi Arabia; it's also religious conservatives who have set up an online version of the Committee for the Promotion of Virtue and the Prevention of Vice. Not that the Saudi government disapproves of such online "activism"; the mutual empowerment between the state and the civil society does not always lead to liberalization. Similarly, Russian nationalist groups are very excited about organizing cyber-attacks on foreign governments and even using online maps to show locations of ethnic minorities in Russian towns. While Sen. Lugar's op-ed lauded a new U.S.-backed mobile-phone-based system for Mexican citizens to report crimes, it failed to mention that Twitter users in Mexico use the site to share information about police checkpoints in their areas so that drunk drivers may avoid arrest.

What we don't seem to realize is that some civil associations, undoubtedly greatly empowered by the Internet, may work toward rather uncivil ends. Instead, we cling to a very outdated view that, as far as authoritarian governments are concerned, all non-state power is good and inevitably leads to democracy, while state power is evil and always leads to suppression. Based on this logic, we often arrive at the paradoxical conclusion that it's okay to scream "Fire!" in a crowded theater, as long as that theater belongs to the Chinese Communist Party or Iran's Supreme Leader.

Despite these caveats, it would be unreasonable for the American government to simply abandon all efforts to use the Internet for promoting democracy abroad. A good starting point is to stop thwarting America's own technology companies, which currently need a host of waivers from the U.S. Treasury's Office of Foreign Assets Control (OFAC) to export Internet services to authoritarian countries (often the target of government sanctions). The reason Microsoft's Messenger is unavailable in Iran is not because the Iranian government hates it, but because Microsoft would need to fight an uphill battle in Washington to bypass the numerous restrictions imposed by OFAC to make that happen, and the poor commercial appeal of places like Iran, North Korea or Cuba makes such fights very costly. Similarly, a host of American hacktivists who wanted to assist the Green Movement with anti-censorship and anti-surveillance technology have also found themselves paralyzed by these sanctions.

This is certainly not a good way to promote "Internet freedom." Resolving such arcane policy disputes is likely to advance American interests abroad more effectively than the flashy and media-friendly undertakings during the June protests in Iran—of which American diplomats have grown so increasingly fond. The growing coziness between them and the top executives of America's leading technology companies, epitomized by state dinners and joint trips to countries like Russia and Iraq, is also a cause for concern. (And flashy such trips really are: The recent delegation to Russia was spearheaded by such a distinguished American technology authority as Ashton Kutcher; why are American taxpayers paying for that once again?) It is certainly a good thing that Obama's youthful bureaucrats have bonded with the brightest creative minds of Silicon Valley. However, the kind of message that it sends to the rest of the world—i.e. that Google, Facebook and Twitter are now just extensions of the U.S. State Department—may simply endanger the lives of those who use such services in authoritarian countries. It's hardly surprising that the Iranian government has begun to view all Twitter users with the utmost suspicion; everyone is now guilty by default.

But there is a broader lesson for the Obama administration here: Diplomacy is, perhaps, one element of the U.S. government that should not be subject to the demands of "open government"; whenever it works, it is usually because it is done behind closed doors. But this may be increasingly hard to achieve in the age of Twittering bureaucrats.

FOURTEEN

Social Networking Is a Temporary Trend

Peter Schwartz

> Peter Schwartz is the president of Knowledge Mosaic, Inc., an online database. In the following article he argues that people are becoming bored and annoyed with social networking. As social networks grow to add more users, Schwartz says they have lost an exclusivity that initially made them alluring and exciting. They have also lost focus and quality: Schwartz says that most social media platforms fail to appeal to a distinct audience and have become diluted with low-quality content. Furthermore, Schwartz says very few people would be willing to pay to access social networks, and if they are not profitable, Schwartz says they will not survive. For all these reasons Schwartz predicts that social networking in its current form will not survive.

It is safe now to say that "Web 2.0" is dead. The evidence is irrefutable and it exposes the twin fallacies the concept of Web 2.0 has depended upon: 1) that people can build their worlds around—indeed, will want to build their worlds around—social networking; and 2) that social networking offers a viable, massively scalable business model.

Let's begin with Facebook, the most popular social networking website in the world. With more than 120 million members, and

60 billion monthly page views, the website is expanding at a white-hot rate. At any given time, students are facebooking each other around the world—in more than 30 languages (with user-created translated editions of the site)—thousands of times per second. While not yet profitable, Facebook has achieved in only four years the signifier of a premium brand—it is now a verb.

A recipient of almost $350 million in equity funding (and another $240 million in debt funding), Facebook charmed the technocracy in 2007 when Microsoft purchased a 1.6 percent stake for $246 million, valuing the company at more than $15 billion. Now, as we close the books on 2008, one might wonder if Facebook is actually worth anything.

We Are Burning Out on Facebook

The company has grown rapidly by any measure, with estimated 2008 revenues of nearly $300 million. From zero to $300 million in four years is nothing to sneeze at. But the company is burning through cash much more quickly than it can replenish its coffers. Its electricity, bandwidth, data storage, and personnel costs are immense. The company needs to buy 50,000 servers alone in 2008 and 2009 to manage its traffic and storage needs.

At the same time, the economy—and advertising rates for banner ads—have fallen off a cliff. Facebook has grown overly dependent on international growth—with 3 out of 4 users from outside the United States. Foreign use is expensive to support and generates little revenue. And so the rumor mill churns with stories of the company's financial quandary. Will Facebook run out of cash? Has it grown too large for US corporations, private equity funds, and venture funds to finance? Can it go public? Why is Facebook CFO Gideon Yu in Dubai? Is a sovereign wealth fund [a state-owned investment fund] the only cash option for Facebook at this point? Is Facebook itself staring into the gun barrel of the largest financing down-round in history?

Facebook's problem is not simply that it cannot grow revenues rapidly enough. Facebook confronts the challenge that aggrieves any social network creating a virtual reality for building and

Americans Are Not Enthralled with Social Networking

A 2009 Pew Research Center poll found that of all the major technological innovations of the twenty-first century, Americans are least impressed with social networking sites and blogs. The fewest number of Americans said these platforms have changed society for the better, and most thought they have not made that much difference in their lives.

Question:
"Have the following innovations been a change for the better, a change for the worse, or have they not made much difference?"

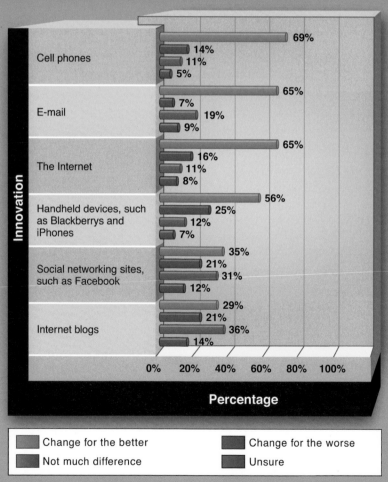

Change for the better | Change for the worse
Not much difference | Unsure

Taken from: Pew Research Center Poll. December 9–13, 2009.

sustaining human relationships. That challenge is Burnout, the acrid smell of neurons frying, and eventually a longing to return to the wholeness of the physical world.

Social Networks Are Becoming Boring and Annoying

Some examples. My 17-year-old son uses Facebook 2–3 hours a day, switching back and forth between FB [Facebook], ESPN, YouTube, Gmail, Google Docs, and iTunes with the smooth, liquid lightning of a boy who has manipulated game controllers for more than a decade. He loves Facebook. He depends on it for

The author says that some Facebook users have become bored with social networking because it has become less inclusive, less interesting, and more annoying.

a vast amount of communication, self-expression, entertainment, and bonding with his peers. But I asked him if he would be willing to pay any amount of money for an annual subscription to Facebook. He paused, and then finally said, "I dunno. Maybe $50. Max."

Kids are turning off to Facebook. Two of my son's friends have deactivated their accounts. They realized that they had too many "friends" whom they did not actually know. They found themselves clicking aimlessly from page to page for too many hours at a time. They got bored. They missed books and movies and the peaceful white space in their lives that Facebook (not to mention MySpace) is so bent on filling in with user-generated "content."

They grew up.

And one day, my son will, too. As Facebook has percolated down to kids in high school (and now even to middle school) and bubbled up to parents who are now themselves "friends" with the friends of their children and spread to every corner of the globe, it has become less exclusive, less interesting, more overwhelming, and ultimately more annoying.

The problem with Facebook is that it feeds on trivia, and in the process has become trivial itself.

Facebook Is Not Worth Much to Users

What, in the end, will people pay for trivia? Very little. At my behest, my son polled his friends and asked them what they would pay for an annual subscription to Facebook. He asked 9 boys and 6 girls. Remember, these are high school juniors and seniors, the sweet spot of the Facebook market. In this sample, 5 kids said they would not pay anything. Another 6 said they would not pay more than a dollar a month. The most anyone would say Facebook was worth to them was $50 annually. Wanting, as always, to fit in, my son reduced his own payment limit to $25 as he reported these results.

This creates a major problem for Facebook, and for other Web 2.0 social networks. The problem is commitment. Facebook has created loyalty without value, quantity that drowns quality. Who can say that MySpace or adult versions of Facebook such as LinkedIn are any different?

Social Networks Suffer from Lack of Quality

During the election, the addictive and massively popular political site, Pollster.com, disabled its comments feature. Mark Blumenthal simply could no longer accept the assault of abusive, insulting, and profane comments of anonymous posters to the website. And this is the problem with Web 2.0. There is no filter for quality. Websites built around or dependent upon user-generated content all too often resemble online versions of talk radio.

Web 2.0 will die. The universal social networks that are its public face cannot survive because they cannot propagate a sustainable user base willing to pay for its services. Remember America Online [AOL]? Netscape killed it (and so AOL killed Netscape). Facebook is nothing more than a new version of America Online, with lots of calories but not much nutrition.

If Web 2.0 dies, it will nonetheless leave a remarkable legacy. Social information and knowledge sharing technologies such as those one finds on Wikipedia, Amazon, Flickr, and even the *New York Times* website are incredibly efficient ways to harvest useful opinion and knowledge. Product reviews on Amazon pool valuable user experiences with specific products (although typically not with books, where Amazon book reviews can suffer from the same oversaturation as Facebook—consider this reflection on the mixed reception from Amazon readers of Jonathan Franzen's bestselling literary novel, *The Corrections*).

Without Focus, Social Networks Suffer

Flickr lets anyone travel the world while sitting in bed with a laptop computer (want to see 666,000 photos of Iceland?). And Manhola Dargis's November 21 [2008] review of the creepily chaste vampire movie, *Twilight*, elicited more than 1,000 reader responses when she solicited their opinions about the scariest movie of all time.

The lesson is clear. Social information and communication requires targeted aim, meaningful purpose, and self-correcting standards of quality. Universal social networks such as Facebook almost by definition, cannot maintain this focus. For this reason, they cannot survive in their current form.

FIFTEEN

Twitter Will Endure

David Carr

In the following viewpoint David Carr explains why he believes Twitter is here to stay. He explains that despite the platform's worst qualities—its silly name, the quantity of information it contains, and the shortness of Tweets—Twitter will likely endure as a communication medium. Carr says that Twitter is a surprisingly efficient way to deliver important and valuable information. He argues that being able to deliver short, newsbreaking bits of information to a mass audience is increasingly useful, meaningful, politically relevant, and even profitable. For these reasons he predicts Twitter will become a permanent part of the Internet.

Carr is a reporter for the culture section of the *New York Times* and the Media Equation columnist for the business section.

I can remember when I first thought seriously about Twitter. Last March, I was at the SXSW conference, a conclave in Austin, Tex., where technology, media and music are mashed up and re-imagined, and, not so coincidentally, where Twitter first rolled out in 2007. As someone who was oversubscribed on Facebook, overwhelmed by the computer-generated RSS feeds of news that came flying at me, and swamped by incoming e-mail messages, the last thing I wanted was one more Web-borne intrusion into my life.

And then there was the name. Twitter.

In the pantheon of digital nomenclature—brands within a sector of the economy that grew so fast that all the sensible names were quickly taken—it would be hard to come up with a noun more trite than Twitter. It impugns itself, promising something slight and inconsequential, yet another way to make hours disappear and have nothing to show for it. And just in case the noun is not sufficiently indicting, the verb, "to tweet" is even more embarrassing.

Beyond the dippy lingo, the idea that something intelligent, something worthy of mindshare, might occur in the space of 140 characters—Twitter's parameters were set by what would fit in a text message on a phone—seems unlikely.

But it was clear that at the conference, the primary news platform was Twitter, with real-time annotation of the panels on stage and critical updates about what was happening elsewhere at a very hectic convention. At 52, I succumbed, partly out of professional necessity.

And now, nearly a year later, has Twitter turned my brain to mush? No, I'm in narrative on more things in a given moment than I ever thought possible, and instead of spending a half-hour surfing in search of illumination, I get a sense of the day's news and how people are reacting to it in the time that it takes to wait for coffee at Starbucks. Yes, I worry about my ability to think long thoughts—where was I, anyway?—but the tradeoff has been worth it.

Some time soon, the company won't say when, the 100-millionth person will have signed on to Twitter to follow and be followed by friends and strangers. That may sound like a MySpace waiting to happen—remember MySpace?—but I'm convinced Twitter is here to stay.

And I'm not alone.

"The history of the Internet suggests that there have been cool Web sites that go in and out of fashion and then there have been open standards that become plumbing," said Steven Johnson, the author and technology observer who wrote a seminal piece about

Twitter, despite its silly name and the dubious quality of tweeted information, is considered by many to be vital to future communications because it is easily accessible through iPads and cell phones.

Twitter for *Time* last June. "Twitter is looking more and more like plumbing, and plumbing is eternal."

Really? What could anyone possibly find useful in this cacophony of short-burst communication?

Well, that depends on whom you ask, but more importantly whom you follow. On Twitter, anyone may follow anyone, but there is very little expectation of reciprocity. By carefully curating the people you follow, Twitter becomes an always-on data stream from really bright people in their respective fields, whose tweets are often full of links to incredibly vital, timely information.

The most frequent objection to Twitter is a predictable one: "I don't need to know someone is eating a donut right now." But if that someone is a serious user of Twitter, she or he might actually be eating the curmudgeon's lunch, racing ahead with a clear, up-to-the-second picture of an increasingly connected, busy world. The service has obvious utility for a journalist, but no matter what business you are in, imagine knowing what the thought leaders in your industry were reading and considering. And beyond following specific individuals, Twitter hash tags allow you to go deep into interests and obsession: #rollerderby, #physics, #puppets and #Avatar, to name just a few of many thousands.

The act of publishing on Twitter is so friction-free—few keystrokes and hit send—that you can forget that others are out there listening. I was on a Virgin America cross-country flight, and used its wireless connection to tweet about the fact that the guy next to me seemed to be the leader of a cult involving Axe body spray. A half-hour later, a steward approached me and said he wondered if I would be more comfortable with a seat in the bulkhead. (He turned out to be a great guy, but I was doing a story involving another part of the company, so I had to decline the offer. @VirginAmerica, its corporate Twitter account, sent me a message afterward saying perhaps it should develop a screening process for Axe. It was creepy and comforting all at once.)

Like many newbies on Twitter, I vastly overestimated the importance of broadcasting on Twitter and after a while, I realized that I was not Moses and neither Twitter nor its users were wondering what I thought. Nearly a year in, I've come to understand that the real value of the service is listening to a wired collective voice.

Not that long ago, I was at a conference at Yale and looked at the sea of open laptops in the seats in front of me. So why wasn't my laptop open? Because I follow people on Twitter who serve as my Web-crawling proxies, each of them tweeting links that I could examine and read on a Blackberry. Regardless of where I am, I surf far less than I used to.

At first, Twitter can be overwhelming, but think of it as a river of data rushing past that I dip a cup into every once in a while. Much of what I need to know is in that cup: if it looks like Apple is going to demo its new tablet, or Amazon sold more Kindles than

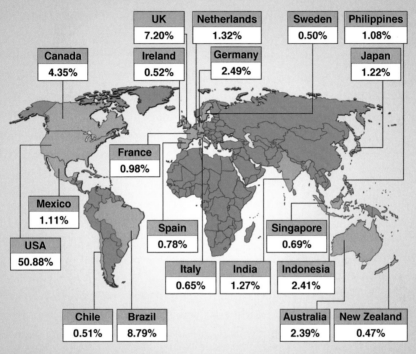

Tweets Heard 'Round the World

As of April 2010, more than 100 million people used Twitter to send billions of Tweets. The majority of Twitter users live in the United States, but the social network is gaining popularity in other countries

UK 7.20%	**Netherlands** 1.32%	**Sweden** 0.50%
		Philippines 1.08%
Canada 4.35%	**Ireland** 0.52%	**Germany** 2.49%
		Japan 1.22%

France 0.98%

Mexico 1.11%

Spain 0.78%

Singapore 0.69%

USA 50.88%

Italy 0.65%   **India** 1.27%   **Indonesia** 2.41%

Chile 0.51%   **Brazil** 8.79%

Australia 2.39%   **New Zealand** 0.47%

Taken from: Sysomos.com, 2010.

actual books at Christmas, or the final vote in the Senate gets locked in on health care, I almost always learn about it first on Twitter.

The expressive limits of a kind of narrative developed from text messages, with less space to digress or explain than this sentence, has significant upsides. The best people on Twitter communicate with economy and precision, with each element—links, hash tags and comments—freighted with meaning. Professional acquaintances whom I find insufferable on every other platform suddenly become interesting within the confines of Twitter.

Twitter is incredibly customizable, with little of the social expectations that go with Facebook. Depending on whom you follow, Twitter can reveal a nation riveted by the last episode of "Jersey Shore" or a short-form conclave of brilliance. There is plenty of nonsense—#Tiger had quite a run—but there are rich threads on the day's news and bravura solo performances from learned autodidacts. And the ethos of Twitter, which is based on self-defining groups, is far more well-mannered than many parts of the Web—more Toastmasters than mosh pit. On Twitter, you are your avatar and your avatar is you, so best not to act like a lout and when people want to flame you for something you said, they are responding to their own followers, not yours, so trolls quickly lose interest.

"Anything that is useful to both dissidents in Iran and Martha Stewart has a lot going for it; Twitter has more raw capability for users than anything since e-mail," said Clay Shirky, who wrote "Here Comes Everybody," a book about social media. "It will be hard to wait out Twitter because it is lightweight, endlessly useful and gets better as more people use it. Brands are using it, institutions are using it, and it is becoming a place where a lot of important conversations are being held."

Twitter helps define what is important by what Mr. Shirky has called "algorithmic authority," meaning that if all kinds of people are pointing at the same thing at the same instant, it must be a pretty big deal.

Beyond the throbbing networked intelligence, there is the possibility of practical magic. Twitter can tell you what kind of netbook you should buy for your wife for Christmas—thanks Twitter!—or call you out when you complain about the long lines it took to buy it, as a tweeter on behalf of the electronics store B & H did when I shared the experience on my Blackberry while in line. I have found transcendent tacos at a car wash in San Antonio, rediscovered a brand of reporter's notepad I adore, uncovered sources for stories, all just by typing a query into Twitter.

All those riches do not come at zero cost: If you think e-mail and surfing can make time disappear, wait until you get ahold of

Twitter, or more likely, it gets ahold of you. There is always something more interesting on Twitter than whatever you happen to be working on.

But in the right circumstance, Twitter can flex some big muscles. Think of last weekend, a heavy travel period marked by a terrorist incident on Friday. As news outlets were scrambling to understand the implications for travelers on Saturday morning, Twitter began lighting up with reports of new security initiatives, including one from @CharleneLi, a consultant who tweeted from the Montreal airport at about 7:30 a.m.: "New security rules for int'l flights into US. 1 bag, no electronics the ENTIRE flight, no getting up last hour of flight."

It was far from the whole story and getting ahead of the news by some hours would seem like no big deal, but imagine you or someone you loved was flying later that same day: Twitter might seem very useful.

Twitter's growing informational hegemony is not assured. There have been serious outages in recent weeks, leading many business and government users to wonder about the stability of the platform. And this being the Web, many smart folks are plotting ways to turn Twitter into so much pixilated mist. But I don't think so. I can go anywhere I want on the Web, but there is no guarantee that my Twitter gang will come with me. I may have quite a few followers, but that doesn't make me Moses.

What You Should Know About Social Networking

What Social Networking Is

- Social networking occurs via Web-based sites or services that allow people to create a personal profile and then communicate or share content with other users of the site or service.
- Site users may form or join groups—based on friend or family connections, school, language, beliefs, or any other shared interest—to meet new people or to keep in touch with people they already know.
- How much and what kind of personal information site users disclose in their profile varies widely. Some want anonymity and disclose as little as possible. Without face-to-face interaction, others feel free to disclose thoughts, feelings, personal likes and dislikes, and detailed descriptions of their activities.
- How "public" a person's profile is—that is, how much of the user's profile can be viewed, commented on, collected, and reposted by other people, inside and outside the network—depends on what the social network site allows and what settings the user chooses.

Types of Social Networking

- Online social communities such as Facebook, LinkedIn, Friendster, and MySpace are what most people think of when they hear "social networking." Users exchange information, gossip, news, photos, music and video, resumes, and messages, much as they do when they talk on the phone or send an e-mail. The difference, in the case of Facebook, is that messaging is instantaneous and can be delivered wherever the recipient happens to be, via whatever device is convenient for the sender: text message, chat, or e-mail.

- Blogs (for example, WordPress and Blogger) are personal online journals, updated frequently and often containing text, images, and links to other blogs. Most blogs are interactive, or designed to allow visitors to leave comments and followers to be alerted when a new blog post appears.
- Microblogs (for example, Tumblr, Twitter) are Web services that allow users to broadcast messages in very short posts (in the case of Twitter, in 140-character-long "tweets") via cell phone or computer.
- Wikis are collaborative social networking sites; that is, websites that allow anyone visiting the site to create and edit the content of the site. The free online encyclopedia Wikipedia is the best-known wiki.
- Multimedia: Some social networking sites are online communities of people who want to share and view not text but video, photography, and art. The best-known video-sharing sites are YouTube, Vimeo, and Hulu. Skype and Livestream are video network services that allow users to see and hear each other in real time, called a livecast, over their computers. People can share, organize, and comment on photographs and other images at sites such as Flikr, Picasa, and FFFOUND!
- Virtual worlds such as Second Life, Habbo, and FarmVille are a form of social networking based on creating an identity called an avatar, representing the user, that exists as an animated character interacting with other avatars in a gamelike digital world.

Who Uses Social Networks

- In 2010 the world's population spent more than 700 billion minutes on social networks and blog sites each month, one out of four American page views on the Internet, according to *Time* magazine, which named Facebook's twenty-six-year-old founder Mark Zuckerberg its 2010 Person of the Year.

- Facebook announced 550 million active users as of December 2010. According to a BBC report, about 30 percent of these users are in the United States, where Facebook is second only to Google in website popularity.
- Twitter reports 105 million registered users, a figure growing by 30,000 people per day. The number of Twitter users who actually tweet is rising too, from 5,000 times a day in 2007, to 300,000 tweets per day in 2008, to 2.5 million per day in 2009, to 50 million tweets per day in 2010 (an average of 600 tweets per second).
- The future users of social networking sites are likely to include many more businesses. A 2010 SaleSpider poll found that 75 percent of small- and medium-size businesses plan to increase their marketing on social networking sites in 2011.
- Ninety-one percent of people who connect to the Internet via a mobile device use social networks, compared with 79 percent of desktop computer users, according to a 2010 Read Write Web report.
- In April 2010 the Pew Research Center reported that half of Americans aged twelve to seventeen send at least fifty text messages a day, and two-thirds said they were more likely to use their phones to text their friends than call them.

According to the 2010 Kaiser Family Foundation study *Generation M^2: Media in the Lives of 8- to 18-Year-Olds*:

- Seventy-five percent of seventh- through twelfth-graders said they had a profile on a social media site.
- Girls spend more time than boys on social networking sites (an average of twenty-five minutes per day for girls versus nineteen minutes per day for boys).
- Seventh- through twelfth-graders spend an average of ninety minutes a day sending or receiving texts on mobile devices.
- Forty-seven percent of adults use social network sites, compared with 73 percent of wired American teens.
- According to a 2010 Retrevo Gadgetology study, the first thing that one-third of women aged eighteen to thirty-four do in the morning is check Facebook; they do this even before going to the bathroom. Of the women in this age group, 21 percent check Facebook in the middle of the night.

- Thirteen percent of Americans aged sixty-five and older log in to a Facebook account each day, a Pew Research Center report noted in May 2010, double the percentage of seniors in 2009.
- Oxford University professor Robin Dunbar objects to the idea that users of social networking sites can maintain online relationships with hundreds of people. Dunbar has a theory that, throughout history, the human brain can only manage about 150 friendships. When he studied social networking sites to see if this limit was rising, he found it was not: Users may like "friending" many hundreds of people, but actual traffic shows users interact with the same circle of 150 people on the web, just as in real life.
- Twenty-four hours of video are uploaded to YouTube every minute, according to a 2010 YouTube factsheet.
- In late 2010 the number of registered users of virtual world sites broke the 1 billion mark, according to business analysts KZero. Of these users, 468 million are between the ages of 10 and 15; the second-largest group is between the ages of 15 and 25.

What You Should Do About Social Networking

Current technology allows access to online social networks, and exploration of new communities, nearly anywhere at any time. But the anonymity of cyberspace and the easy intimacy of cyberspace are both illusions. Along with the great innovation and opportunity of social networking sites come new codes of conduct, new risks, and new ways of dealing with those risks.

Learn and Practice Social Networking Etiquette

Social networking etiquette boils down to the golden rule of behavior in all environments: Treat others as you wish to be treated. This means refraining from posting negative status updates, spreading gossip or rumors, or making threats online. Do not make public IMs, text messages, or e-mail that was intended to be private. People and relationships change, and you may unfriend someone or be unfriended by someone you once shared sensitive information with or about. Keep all content you post online positive. The terms of use agreement you sign automatically when you register on a site is full of provisions for legal penalties for defamation; that is, for posting a false statement about someone that harms her reputation. Do not post or upload copyrighted material; the terms of use agreement holds you legally liable for copyright infringement too.

Do take advantage of the opportunity to show artistic talents and experiment with other creative content on a profile or blog. Venturing out of your comfort zone artistically and academically is a way to interact with others who share your interests, who can give you constructive feedback, and who can introduce you to new interests.

Protect Your Privacy

The Children's Online Privacy Protection Act (COPPA) bans online sites and services from collecting information from users or visitors under the age of thirteen without a parent's permission. Many underage children get around the ban, however, simply by giving a false birth date and joining in social networking activities. Know that this is a violation of the site's usage terms and has consequences. If you are unaware of the privacy risks of social networking, through age or inexperience, follow these Federal Trade Commission tips for socializing safely online:

- Restrict access to your page to a carefully chosen group of people; for example, friends from your school, team, or family. Never post your full name, Social Security number, address, phone number, or bank or credit card numbers online. Do not post other people's information, either, or photographs that could be an invasion of someone else's privacy. Choose a screen name that does not reveal too many personal details; it should not include your name, age, or hometown.
- Use social networking sites that have secure privacy settings, and consider choosing a private profile that only friends can see. Then be careful about whom you admit as a friend, and keep your password to yourself. Do not assume that people are who they claim to be. Online anonymity entices some people to create fictional identities and make friends under false pretenses.
- Even if you choose privacy settings carefully, remember that there is no such thing as a private social media site. When you post a message or information online, you cannot permanently delete or take it back. Search engines can bring up your posts years later. So only post information, photographs, videos, jokes, and messages you would not mind being seen by your parents, teachers, college admissions officers, employers, or the police.

Set Healthy Limits

In April 2010, two hundred University of Maryland students were challenged to go twenty-four hours without social media. No texting or IM-ing, no iPhones, no laptops, e-mail, Facebook, or Twitter. Researchers were shocked by the high number of students who reported feeling miserable—jittery and irritable, as if they were having physical withdrawal symptoms—less than six hours into the test. Nearly all had to fight the urge to check for messages. By the end of the experiment, many participants admitted they were "incredibly addicted to media" and in need of limits. The following tips can help you set healthy limits to avoid becoming dependent on social networking.

If you do not know someone well (or at all), do not feel pressured to friend or follow him or her. Before you approve a friend request, make sure the person has a genuine connection to you, such as a real-life friend in common. *Social Times* blogger Raj Dash sets another condition for keeping it real before friending someone new: The person "has to display a real profile pic, not an avatar, photo of an inanimate object, or some random starlet." Likewise, do not be offended if someone does not respond to your friend request, and do not ask more than once.

Schedule your social networking time, and limit it to no more than thirty to sixty minutes a day, total. Do not leave Facebook open in a browser tab while you are doing something else on the computer; it is too easily distracting. Also avoid fiddling with your profile; changing your profile image again and again or frequently changing your status is a sign that you are too wrapped up in social media. Balanced use of social networking means the media serve your needs, not the other way around.

ORGANIZATIONS TO CONTACT

The editors have compiled the following list of organizations concerned with the issues debated in this book. The descriptions are derived from materials provided by the organizations. All have publications or information available for interested readers. The list was compiled on the date of publication of the present volume; names, addresses, phone and fax numbers, and e-mail and Internet addresses may change. Be aware that many organizations take several weeks or longer to respond to inquiries, so allow as much time as possible.

Berkman Center for Internet & Society
Harvard University
23 Everett St., 2nd Fl., Cambridge, MA 02138
(617) 495-7547
fax: (617) 495-7641
e-mail: cyber@law.harvard.edu
website: http://cyber.law.harvard.edu

Founded in 1997, the Berkman Center for Internet and Society is dedicated to the study of the Internet and its effects on politics, law, and culture. Among its many projects is Digital Natives, which studies the Internet use of a generation "born digital"; that is, young people who have been using (and creating) digital media all their lives. Publications available on the website include "Why Youth Heart Social Network Sites," "Sexting: Youth Practices and Legal Implications," and the 2010 report *Youth, Privacy, and Reputation*.

Center for Democracy and Technology (CDT)
1634 I St. NW, Ste. 1100, Washington, DC 20006
(202) 637-9800
fax: (202) 637-0968
e-mail: info@cdt.org
website: www.cdt.org

The mission of CDT is to develop public policy solutions that advance constitutional civil liberties and democratic values in new computer and communications media. Pursuing its mission through policy research, public education, and coalition building, the center works to increase citizens' privacy and the public's control over the use of personal information held by government and other institutions. Its publications include issue briefs, policy papers, and *CDT Policy Posts*, an online, occasional publication that covers issues regarding the civil liberties of those using the information highway.

Center for Safe and Responsible Internet Use
474 W. 29th Ave., Eugene, OR 97405
(541) 556-1145
e-mail: contact@csriu.org
website: www.cyberbully.org

The Center for Safe and Responsible Internet Use was founded in 2002 by Nancy Willard, an expert on student Internet-use management in schools and the author of *Cyberbullying and Cyberthreats*. In addition to briefs and guides for educators and parents, the center offers numerous reports, articles, and books for student researchers, including "Sexting and Youth" and *Cyber-Safe Kids, Cyber-Savvy Teens*. The site also offers a social networking code for young people called the DigiDesiderata, with rules such as "If you compare your profile and number of friends with others, you may mistakenly think you are 'hot' or 'not.' Seek quality, not quantity, in your online friending."

Consortium for School Networking (CoSN)
1025 Vermont Ave. NW, Ste. 1010, Washington, DC 20005
(202) 861-2676 or (866) 267-8747
fax: (202) 393-2011
website: www.cosn.org

Founded in 1992, CoSN is a nonprofit organization that advocates and develops ways of using Internet technologies to improve teaching and learning in grades kindergarten through twelve (K-12). It supports the use of open-source software in schools to foster collaboration and allow teachers to modify and share their applications. The consortium publishes reports such as *Hot Technologies for K-12 Schools* and "Web 2.0 in Education," which argues that schools must integrate social networking and participatory media or be left behind.

Creative Commons
171 Second St., Ste. 300, San Francisco, CA 94105
(415) 369-8480
fax: (415) 278-9419
website: http://creativecommons.org

Creative Commons, a nonprofit organization founded in 2001, works to increase the amount of creative content (artistic, educational, and scientific) in "the commons"—that is, available to the public for free and legal use. It works alongside copyright, issuing free licenses to mark a work with the freedom the creator wants it to carry, so others can legally copy, share, remix, use commercially, or repurpose it. By 2008 more than 130 million works had been released under Creative Commons licenses on such well-known platforms as Google, Flickr, PLoS, and Wikipedia. The Creative Commons website offers links to free works and explanation of how licensed works may and may not be used.

Electronic Frontier Foundation (EFF)
454 Shotwell St., San Francisco, CA 94110-1914
(415) 436-9333
e-mail: information@eff.org
website: www.eff.org

EFF is an organization of students and other individuals that aims to promote a better understanding of telecommunications issues. It fosters awareness of civil liberties issues arising from advancements in computer-based communications media and supports litigation to preserve, protect, and extend First Amendment rights in computing and telecommunications technologies.

Electronic Privacy Information Center (EPIC)
1718 Connecticut Ave. NW, Ste. 200, Washington, DC 20009
(202) 483-1140

fax: (202) 483-1248
website: http://epic.org

EPIC is a public interest research center founded in 1994 to raise public awareness of civil liberties issues related to new digital technologies and the Internet. It works to protect privacy and strengthen First Amendment rights. One example is its May 2010 complaint to the Federal Trade Commission that forced Facebook to enhance its privacy controls. EPIC publishes the online newsletter *EPIC Alert*. The website offers pages on topics such as cloud computing, social networking, Google Streets, and children's online privacy.

Federal Trade Commission (FTC)
Consumer Response Center
600 Pennsylvania Ave. NW, Washington, DC 20580
(877) 382-4357
website: www.ftc.gov/bcp/menus/consumer/entertain.shtm

The FTC, created in 1914, is the consumer protection agency of the federal government. It investigates unfair and illegal business practices and identity theft on the Internet. Its Consumers & the Internet site explains user rights and risks regarding Internet access, computer privacy and security, spare, and P2P (peer-to-peer) file sharing. Website resources include numerous publications about secure use of new digital technologies, including "Social Networking Sites: Safety Tips for Tweens and Teens."

Internet Education Foundation
Center for Democracy and Technology
1634 I St. NW, Ste. 1100, Washington, DC 20006
(202) 638-4370
fax: (202) 637-0968
e-mail: tim@neted.org
website: www.neted.org

Founded in 1996, the Internet Education Foundation is a nonprofit public interest group that works to educate and lobby policy makers and legislators in support of free expression and privacy in web technologies. It supports "net neutrality" laws, which concern government regulation of broadband providers to keep them from controlling online "traffic" in an unfair way—for example, by favoring some kinds of transmissions or content over others. Website links include GetNetWise, a toolkit of video tutorials and up-to-date blog posts such as "Are Teens Broadcasting Their Mobile Location on Facebook?" and "A New Social Networking Resource for Families."

Internet Society (ISOC)
1775 Wiehle Ave., Ste. 201, Reston, VA 20190-5108
(703) 439-2120
fax: (703) 326-9881
e-mail: isoc@isoc.org
website: www.isoc.org

The ISOC is an international, nonprofit organization founded in 1992 to help determine what global standards and policies should guide the growth of the Internet. Its goal is to increase the availability and utility of the Internet on the widest possible scale. It is a clearinghouse for Internet information and education and runs training programs for setting up Internet connections and digital literacy in developing countries. Useful website resources include a history of the Internet, guidelines on the Internet code of conduct, and good descriptions of Internet infrastructure: how the web is organized, how IP Internet protocol and domain names are managed, and what bodies are responsible for operations and security.

Kaiser Family Foundation
1330 G St. NW, Washington, DC 20005
(202) 347-5270
fax: (202) 347-5274
website: www.kff.org

The foundation is a nonprofit research organization focusing on health care issues. It also serves as a clearinghouse of public health information in the United States. Its Media and Health website offers the 2010 report *Generation M^2: Media in the Lives of 8- to 18-Year-Olds*, a comprehensive national survey that charts the rise and effects of social media use among American youth from 1999 through 2009. Other useful resources available on the website include the report *The Teen Media Juggling Act: Media Multitasking Among American Youth.*

National Middle School Association (NMSA)
4151 Executive Pkwy., Ste. 300, Westerville, OH 43081
(614) 895-4730 or (800) 528-6672
fax: (614) 895-4750
e-mail: info@nmsa.org
website: www.nmsa.org

NMSA is an organization of some thirty thousand teachers, college students, parents, and community leaders interested in improving education for middle school students. The association publishes the monthly magazine *Middle Ground*. Especially useful 2010 articles include "Integrating Video Games into the Middle Grades Classroom" and "Tools for Schools: What's New with Web 2.0," which describes and provides links to more than twenty tools for classroom use that allow students to produce their own digital content, including ThinkQuest, RSS feeds, the creative programming application Alice, Wordle, and Gabcast. This and many other publications are available on the website.

The Progress & Freedom Foundation
1444 I St. NW, Washington, DC, 20005
(202) 289-8928
fax: (202) 289-6079
e-mail: mail@pff.org
website: www.pff.org

The Progress & Freedom Foundation studies the digital revolution and its implications for public policy. Its mission is to educate policy makers, opinion leaders, and the public about issues associated with technological change, based on a philosophy of limited government, free markets, and individual sovereignty.

P2P Foundation
+31 20 772 8781

e-mail: michelsub2004@gmail.com
website: http://p2pfoundation.net

Part wiki, part blog, part social network, P2P (Peer-to-Peer) is a nonprofit organization founded by Michael Bauwens in the Netherlands. It is dedicated to the idea of the web as a worldwide community of users creating, collaborating on, and sharing free content, without advertising or government regulation. It is a clearinghouse of research on peer-to-peer practices and open source content. Its huge catalogs "Open Everything" and "Open Hardware Directory" link to content from complete operating systems such as GNU/Linux to music and books to how-to building projects. As such, it serves as a messy, fascinating example of social networking in action.

Wikimedia Foundation
149 New Montgomery St., 3rd Fl., San Francisco, CA 94105
(415) 839-6885
fax: (415) 882-0495
e-mail: info@wikimedia.org
website: http://wikimediafoundation.org

The foundation is the parent organization of Wikipedia, its best-known project. It is a nonprofit charitable organization dedicated to developing and providing free, multilingual, educational web content. Other projects (all collaboratively developed by users) include Wikimedia Commons, a collection of over 6.7 million free images, videos, and sound files; Wiktionary; Wikiquote; and Wikibooks. The foundation's Press Room offers press releases, statistics, and Q&As about the foundation's operations and philosophy.

BIBLIOGRAPHY

Books

Naomi Baron, *Always On: Language in an Online and Mobile World.* New York: Oxford University Press, 2010.

Mark Bauerlein, *The Dumbest Generation: How the Digital Age Stupefies Young Americans and Jeopardizes Our Future (Or, Don't Trust Anyone Under 30).* New York: Tarcher, 2009.

Frances Jacobson Harris, *I Found It on the Internet: Coming of Age Online.* 2nd ed. Chicago: American Library Association Editions, 2010.

Thomas A. Jacobs, *Teen Cyberbullying Investigated: Where Do Your Rights End and Consequences Begin?* Minneapolis: Free Spirit, 2010.

Todd Kelsey, *Social Networking Spaces: From Facebook to Twitter and Everything in Between.* New York: Apress, 2010.

David Kirkpatrick, *The Facebook Effect: The Inside Story of the Company That Is Connecting the World.* New York: Simon and Schuster, 2010.

Greg Lastowka, *Virtual Justice: The New Laws of Online Worlds.* New Haven, CT: Yale University Press, 2010.

Saul Levmore and Martha C. Nussbaum, eds., *The Offensive Internet: Speech, Privacy, and Reputation.* Cambridge, MA: Harvard University Press, 2011.

John Palfrey, *Born Digital: Understanding the First Generation of Digital Natives.* New York: Basic, 2010.

Clay Shirky, *Here Comes Everybody.* New York: Penguin, 2009.

Deanna Zandt, *Share This! How You Will Change the World with Social Networking.* San Francisco: Berrett-Koehler, 2010.

Periodicals and Internet Sources

David Carr, "How Obama Tapped into Social Networks' Power," *New York Times*, November 9, 2008, p. B1.

Pete Cashmore, "Privacy Is Dead, and Social Media Hold Smoking

Gun," CNN.com, October 28, 2009. http://edition.cnn.com/2009/OPINION/10/28/cashmore.online.privacy.

David Chartier, "Future of Social Media: The Walls Come Crumbling Down," *Wired*, June 2, 2009. www.wired.com/dualper spectives/article/news/2009/06/dp_social_media_ars.

Marco R. della Cava, "Some Ditch Social Networks to Reclaim Time," *USA Today*, February 10, 2010. www.usatoday.com/tech/webguide/internetlife/2010-02-10-1Asocialbacklash10_CV_N.htm.

Julian Dibbell, "Future of Social Media: Is a Tweet the New Size of a Thought?," *Wired*, June 2, 2009. www.wired.com/dualper spectives/article/news/2009/06/dp_social_wired.

Economist, "The Future Is Another Country: Social Networks and Statehood," July 22, 2010.

Kathy English, "Will Twitter Transform Journalism?," *Star* (Toronto, Canada), June 12, 2010. www.thestar.com/opinion/editorial opinion/article/822099–english-will-twitter-transform-jour nalism.

Dan Fletcher, "How Facebook Is Redefining Privacy," *Time*, May 20, 2010.

Neal Gabler, "The Zuckerberg Revolution," *Los Angeles Times*, November 28, 2010.

Guilbert Gates, "Facebook Privacy: A Bewildering Tangle of Options," *New York Times*, May 12, 2010.

Lev Grossman, "Person of the Year 2010: Mark Zuckerberg," *Time*, December 15, 2010.

Kate Harding, "Social Networking Is Not Killing Friendship," Salon.com, December 9, 2009. www.salon.com/life/broadsheet/feature/2009/12/09/facebook_friends.

Laura M. Holson, "Breaking Up in a Digital Fishbowl," *New York Times*, January 6, 2010.

Patti Lane, "ReCaptcha: How to Turn Blather into Books," *Christian Science Monitor*, February 19, 2009.

Tom Meltzer, "Social Networking: Failure to Connect: How Can You Be Lonely When You Have So Many Friends?," *Guardian*, August 7, 2010. www.guardian.co.uk/media/2010/aug/07/social-networking-friends-lonely.

Luisetta Mudie, "Citizen Journalism 'On the Rise,'" Radio Free Asia, May 27, 2010. www.rfa.org/english/news/china/journalism-05272010112657.html.

NOVA scienceNOW, "Profile: Luis von Ahn: Games with a Purpose," PBS, June 30, 2009. www.pbs.org/wgbh/nova/tech/profile-von-ahn.html.

Megan O'Neill, "YouTube and the Future of Citizen Journalism," *Social Times*, June 23, 2010. http://socialtimes.com/youtube-and-the-future-of-citizen-journalism_b15810.

Anna Pickard, "Virtual People, Real Friends," *Guardian* Manchester (UK) January 2, 2009. www.guardian.co.uk/comment isfree/2009/jan/02/internet-relationships.

Ron Steinman, "Citizen Journalism: A Recipe for Disaster," *Digital Journalist*, December 2009. http://digitaljournalist.org/issue 0912/citizen-journalism-a-recipe-for-disaster.html.

Hilary Stout, "Antisocial Networking?," *New York Times*, April 30, 2010.

Tony Woodlief, "Ya Gotta Have (Real) Friends," *Wall Street Journal*, June 12, 2009. http://online.wsj.com/article/SB12447 6939261008701.html.

Sophia Yan, "How to Disappear from Facebook and Twitter," *Time*, January 19, 2010.

INDEX

will endure, 93–99

W

Writing
  by social network users *vs.*

nonusers, 46
  technology builds skill in, 47

Z

Zuckerberg, Mark, 5, *7*, *57*

PICTURE CREDITS